MYTHS AND MYSTERIES

OF

KENTUCKY

TRUE STORIES
OF THE UNSOLVED AND UNEXPLAINED

MIMI O'MALLEY AND SUSAN SAWYER

gPP

Guilford, Connecticut

To my family: Mike, John, Kate, Anne Bourdet, Andre Bourdet,
Emily Bourdet, Bob O'Malley, and Marie O'Malley

In memory of my Ronnie
S. S.

Copyright © 2014 by Morris Book Publishing, LLC

Map by Alena Joy Pearce © Morris Book Publishing, LLC
Project editor: Lauren Szalkiewicz
Layout: Mary Ballachino

Library of Congress Cataloging-in-Publication Data is available on file.

ISBN 978-0-7627-7224-7

Printed in the United States of America

10 9 8 7 6 5 4 3 2 1

CONTENTS

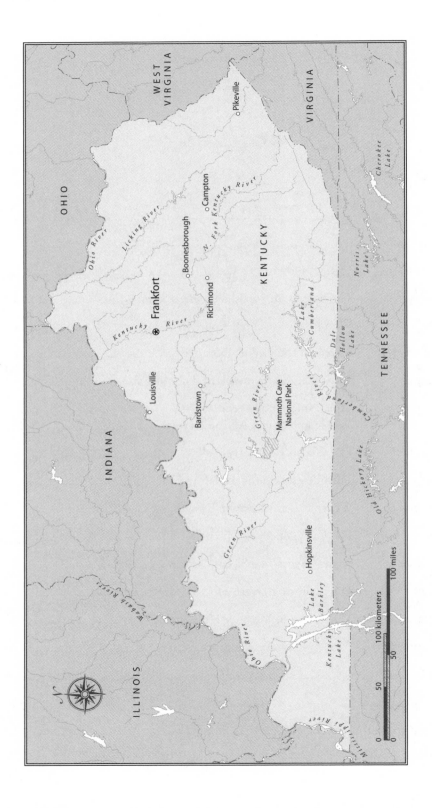

ACKNOWLEDGMENTS

The authors gratefully acknowledge the assistance of Thomas Lisanti, New York Public Library; Jennifer DuPlaga and Becky Riddle, Kentucky Historical Society; Jason Flahardy, University of Kentucky Archives; and Amy Purcell, University of Louisville Special Collections. The authors would like to extend much gratitude to Shannon Gay of The Learning House, Inc., for her expertise on digital technology.

INTRODUCTION

Most people who grew up in the Bluegrass State learned in elementary school that the earliest settlers in Kentucky were Native Americans, followed by colonists seeking religious tolerance and economic prosperity. Who would believe the likelihood that Kentucky's earliest settlers were in fact Norse Welshmen who predate Columbus by three hundred years? Kentucky's bounty of natural resources intrigued more than one sailor, hunter, and soldier. Such a bounty was even more lucrative when it was in the form of a precious metal: silver. Once word reached the colonists along the eastern seaboard that more than just land beckoned beyond the Appalachian Mountains, the secret was no more and the area flooded with settlers. However, American history books detail the tenuous relationship between the pioneers seeking westward expansion and the Native Americans who inhabited Kentucky. Both groups claimed a vested interest in the land called Kentucke, and neither one of them was willing to give in to the other so easily.

The harsh reality of living on the Kentucky frontier meant disease, deception, and even death. Settlements randomly dotting mountain valleys and ravines, rolling knobs, and wooded hillsides were left to fend for themselves. Frontier justice meant every man and woman not only learned to use a weapon, but also used it when he or she saw fit, and both racial diatribes and economic disparity prompted many to yield a weapon. If fearing attack was not enough of a concern, Kentuckians braved unknown diseases that afflicted both man and animal. Eighteenth- and nineteenth-century pharmacology was relegated to homemade remedies and microsurgeries that surely would make any modern practicing physician shudder. According to the philosophy of the time, if such therapies didn't manage to cure an ailment, then surely the affliction must be the result of a freak of nature.

Many of Kentucky's legends and mysteries surround individuals who held their own no matter who they came up against. Mike Fink and Daniel Boone embody the self-made man who maneuvered through life with a swagger, be he a woodsman, soldier, or statesman. And yet there were those Kentuckians who earned notoriety for their skill in executing unimagined human feats, such as the clairvoyant Edgar Cayce. I hope you enjoy reading *Myths & Mysteries of Kentucky,* which highlights the stories of these individuals and historical events.

—Mimi O'Malley

Some time ago I had the joy of living and working in Louisville for several years. My daughter was born in that wonderful city, and I fell in love with the people, the culture, and the beautiful horse country of the Commonwealth. Once you read *Myths &*

Mysteries of Kentucky, I believe you'll fall in love with the appeal of the Bluegrass State, too.

Between stagecoach taverns and palatial mansions, the historic buildings of Kentucky have many secrets hidden within their walls. On the following pages, you'll read about several places that hold mysterious tales from both the past and present. The Old Talbott Tavern in Bardstown, Liberty Hall in Frankfort, Waverly Hills Sanatorium in Louisville, and White Hall in Madison County have rich historical backdrops that make them perfect spots for ghostly spirits to roam.

You'll discover that the dark depths of Mammoth Cave hold puzzling tales, as well. And the events that resulted from the deaths of two Kentucky women—Anne Mitchell and Octavia Hatcher—are guaranteed to send chills down your spine! So grab your favorite drink, sit back, and spend some time with *Myths & Mysteries of Kentucky.* Enjoy!

—Susan Sawyer

CHAPTER 1

The Mystery of the Welsh Indians

American history books teach us that Christopher Columbus discovered America in 1492. But mysterious artifacts discovered in Kentucky predate Columbus by hundreds of years. Is it possible someone other than Columbus may have reached American shores long before the close of the fifteenth century?

In 1799 six skeletons were found in Jeffersonville, Indiana, directly across the Ohio River from Louisville. Attorney, civic leader, and honorary Kentucky colonel Reuben Durrett reported that each of the six skeletons bore a breastplate bearing a mermaid and harp. The symbolism was apparent: the Welsh coat of arms. The harp was the Welsh national musical instrument, and the mermaid indicated the shield bearer was of Welsh descent. Moreover, Durrett noted a gravestone located by the Falls of the Ohio with an inscription of 1186, but the caption was unrecognizable. Whose headstone was this?

Across the river in Kentucky, construction workers stumbled across another remarkable find in preparation for pouring the foundation of a flour mill. As they cut down a huge sycamore with two hundred annular rings, they were astonished to find an iron axe lying under the roots a few feet from the surface. Interestingly, the axe predated English settlers and French explorer Sieur de LaSalle, who did not explore the area until 1670. Two centuries earlier, not even the Native Americans of the region had knowledge of iron smelting at the time. So where did the axe come from?

Another mysterious site in Kentucky was discovered in 1873. Indiana state geologist E. T. Cox and his assistant, William Borden, came upon a stone fort at Devil's Backbone, fourteen miles north of the Falls of the Ohio. Situated on a high rock ridge at the confluence of Fourteen-Mile Creek and the Ohio River, the prehistoric fortification consisted of a limestone wall, 150 feet long, carved along the front and side of the hill. Loose stones were piled along the slope of the hill and then stacked vertically for the last ten feet. The men believed at one point the wall reached a height of seventy-five feet. Atop the hill, inside the fort, the men discovered five mounds. When the mounds were excavated, pieces of charcoal, decomposed bones, and other relics were uncovered. Stone walling of this construction was not typical of Native Americans, so who built this fort?

At the other end of the Falls of the Ohio, a graveyard was discovered that contained the prehistoric remains of hundreds of individuals and fifty tombs cut of roughhewn stone. All of the remains were male, none of who were less than six and a half

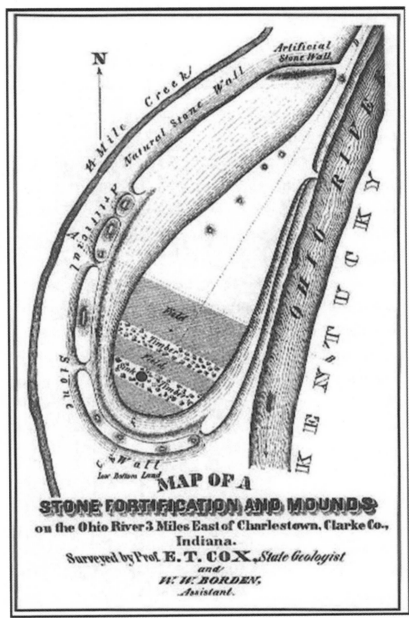

MAP OF A
STONE FORTIFICATION AND MOUNDS
on the Ohio River 3 Miles East of Charlestown, Clarke Co.,
Indiana.
Surveyed by Prof. E. T. COX, State Geologist
and
W. W. BORDEN,
Assistant.

Sketch of fort mounds on the Ohio River in Indiana

feet tall. These men were buried in a sitting position, weapons in their laps, and their heads inclined to face the rising sun. Each man had an indention to the left temple. This discovery bears similarity to ancient head skeletons found in Britain, where the practice of trephinning, or burring a hole in the skull for medical purposes, was common.

In 1963, construction crews working on the Sherman Minton Bridge connecting Louisville to New Albany, Indiana, unearthed a cache of Roman coins dating from AD 235 and 268, during the reign of Maximus I and Claudius II. Why would Roman coins turn up in Kentucky?

All of these unexplainable discoveries allude to the possibility that another group, possibly the Welsh, discovered America more than three hundred years prior to Columbus. If that was the case, what happened to the supposed Welsh settlers? In order to decipher if the Welsh truly explored the interior of America, one needs to examine the story of Madoc and the Welsh Indians. Madoc was a twelfth-century explorer and illegitimate son of Owain Gwynedd, a powerful chieftain in North Wales, and his Irish mistress, Brenda.

By the twelfth century, Wales was divided into three kingdoms: Gwynedd in the north and west, Powys in the east, and Deheubarth in the south. Ascending to the throne in 1138, Owain Gwynedd ruled his principality with a mixture of brutality and sagaciousness. He dealt brutal punishment to those considered disloyal, going so far as to imprison his own son,

Cynan, as well as blinding and castrating a nephew. He warred constantly with his brother, Cadwahr, and his chief rival, Henry II, the Norman king of England, who made multiple attempts to invade and conquer Wales. Although chieftain over one third of Wales, Owain understood Henry II's mission to conquer Wales and sought attempts at unification. He diplomatically garnered an alliance with France against Henry II.

Owain not only assumed the throne from his father, Gruffud ap Cynan, but also inherited his father's love of poetry. Many poets and minstrels traveled from Ireland to Wales regaling not only Owain's military prowess in story and verse, but also his gigantic stature and charisma.

Owain wed two women and sired at least twenty-seven children with various mistresses. His marriage to his first cousin, Chrisiant, was ruled incestuous by the Catholic Church, and Owain was excommunicated by Thomas à Becket, the archbishop of Canterbury. One of his mistresses was Brenda, a daughter of an Irish lord and Viking ancestor, who gave birth to six sons. One of these sons was Madoc, born between 1134 and 1142. Whether covering up his infidelity, salvaging his reputation to religious leaders, or eliminating any claim to the throne, Owain planned to kill the infant Madoc. Another account reports Madoc was born with a clubfoot and such a deformity was considered ill-fated for the heir to the throne. However, Brenda discovered this plan, smuggled Madoc out of Wales, and sent him to Ireland.

Owain died in 1169, plunging the entire province into civil war. The oldest legitimate son, Iorweth, was deemed unfit to rule because of facial deformities. Two other sons, Howell and David, waged war for the succession to the throne. Madoc may have attempted to return to Gwynedd after his father's death, but he must have known his death sentence was assured in Wales. David not only was successful in killing Howell and taking the throne, but also was instrumental in slaying two other brothers. He even issued a death sentence for Madoc's wife, Amnesta, a maiden in his mother's court.

A true product of his Viking forbearers, Madoc grew up to become an experienced sailor while living in Ireland. His sailing acumen was the result of many travels to and from Ireland and Scandinavia to visit family. His exile and naval expertise were relayed in poetry written by Meredith ap Rhys, Guytin Owen, and Lodewijk van Velthem. Realizing any claim to the Welsh throne would preclude him, Madoc decided to venture west by sea. From his Viking ancestors, he knew there were two ways to successfully reach the Americas: The first way was the northern route by Iceland; the second was by the Caribbean trade winds. Madoc took the southern route for his initial voyage, which landed him in Mexico.

This landing was acknowledged by several sources, including the Toltec Indians, who predated the founding of Mexico City in 1325. Their legends discussed giant white men, considered to be gods, arriving on ships with square sails, a typical characteristic of a Viking ship. Furthermore, the speech of Montezuma to his subjects after he was taken prisoner by Cortes in 1520 noted "descendants from a far distant northern nation, whose tongue and manners we yet have partly preserved." And Sebastian Cabot, who discovered Florida and Mexico around 1495, found several parts of the coast inhabited by descendants of the first British voyagers, who had arrived in 1170.

Upon leaving Mexico on friendly terms, Madoc is believed to have sailed up the Gulf of Mexico and into Mobile Bay. Several of Madoc's shipmates disembarked in Mobile Bay, finding the land too inviting to pass by. This initial sailing excursion west was purported to have taken four years.

By the time Madoc reached Wales, he relayed to the Welsh his adventures in Mexico and the virgin land of Mobile Bay. His tales enticed many new settlers, anxious to leave warring Wales, to join him on his next voyage. In 1170 he set sail from north Wales on his second voyage with his two brothers, a sister, and possibly three thousand colonists in as many as eleven ships. His single-mast ships were up to seventy-five feet in length, with deep, straight keels and eight to sixteen pairs of oars. One of Madoc's ships, the *Gwennan Gorn,* was considered magical. Since Madoc believed iron would interfere with his compass, the *Gwennan Gorn* was held together by stag horns rather than nails.

After an approximate two-month voyage, Madoc's ships reached Mobile Bay. Madoc, however, was unable to find the shipmates he had left several months earlier, unaware if they had fallen at the hands of Indians or disease. The ships then turned back into the Gulf of Mexico and made their way back to Wales, stopping at the island of Lundy in the Bristol Channel outside the confines of David and his warring brethren.

While docked in Lundy, Madoc recruited more war-torn settlers and set sail in 1171 in the same ships. In fact two ships from Madoc's expedition, *Gwennan Gorn* and *Pedr Sant,* commanded by his brother Riryd, were noted in the maritime log of *Missing Ships of Britain* in AD 1172. Since Madoc never returned to Wales after this third voyage, it is unknown whether the party made landing in Mobile Bay. However, based on Indian lore, it is suspected he most likely reached the mouth of the Mississippi River.

From this point Madoc's expedition begins to tell two tales. Accounts of supposed "White Indians" in the upper Midwest Dakotas noted their ancestors landed at the mouth of the Mississippi and sailed up the river. Madoc's white colonists were defeated by the Cherokees in Alabama, Tennessee, and Georgia, and fled farther upstream along the Missouri River, eventually settling in North Dakota. As exploration of the Northwest gained fervor in the 1600s and 1700s, explorers, soldiers, and missionaries reported that light-skinned Indians who spoke Welsh inhabited the region. This tribe, named the Mandan, lived a culture reminiscent of Welsh forbearers. French Canadian explorer Pierre Gaultier noted the Mandan lived in villages with streets and squares. Likewise, they had fair skin, spoke a derivation of Welsh, and traveled in tublike canoes similar in construction to Welsh coracles. Tragically, in 1838, smallpox wiped out the Mandan.

Another account counters that Madoc's expedition made its way to the Falls of the Ohio, which prevented any further sailing. Upon disembarking, the party realized the area supported habitation and broke off into small bands, intermarrying with Native Americans. Local tradition claims they built great mounds at various locations along the Ohio River. Realizing they had not left all warring in Wales, the group clashed with the Native peoples, which led them to build stone fortifications such as Devil's Backbone for protection. These long rock walls, pits, and carved caves were reminiscent of similar ones in Wales. In the late eighteenth century, Piankeshaw Chief Tobacco relayed the story of whites clashing with Indians in the Great Battle at Sand Island at the lower end of the Falls of the Ohio to American Revolutionary War hero George Rogers Clark, an older brother to explorer William Clark.

French explorer René-Robert Cavelier, sieur de LaSalle noted as he ventured the Ohio River in 1669 and 1670 that his men abandoned the exploration at the Falls. Their reluctance to continue up the river may be attributed to Shawnee tales that the Falls was haunted by the victims of the Great Battle, which had been fought at the site seven years earlier. At the tail end of the Beaver Wars, which were fought during the mid-1600s, conflict climaxed between the French and Iroquois over trading supplies with the Algonquian. An outgrowth of this tension fueled the Great Battle at the Falls, with the Welsh making a stand against the Indians on Sand Island, near Louisville's Shippingport Island. Only a few Welsh survived. It is speculated some survivors may have escaped to a colony along the Big Creek at Wiggins Point (Indiana), where stone fortresses similar to Rose Island in Clark County, Indiana, were found. Rose Island fortifications contained foxholes and walls stretching thirty-six hundred feet in length. In 1874 geologists discovered human bones protruding from the banks of Big Creek at Wiggins Point, as well as human remains buried in a sitting posture and covered with shells and fragments of pottery. At this location survivors would have been free of Iroquois retaliation, since they could bypass the Ohio River at the Falls via the Wabash River.

Remnants of suspected Welsh inhabitants traverse the Bluegrass State. Stone forts and towers built on earthen mounds in strategic locations dot the Ohio River, starting from the Falls of the Ohio to the mouth of the Great Miami River in southern Ohio. A resident of Vevay, Indiana, once described seven such towers between Carrollton and Warsaw, Kentucky. Each tower sat on a high hill, giving its occupants the ability to send smoke signals upon any emergency. Approximately thirty-five miles upstream, the remains of a village and burial ground of unusually large inhabitants were found in Augusta, Kentucky. Local legend states that a jawbone found in 1790 was so large it could fit over the settler's entire head.

Some contend Madoc was no myth, but an actual explorer who reached North America long before Columbus. Supporters of the Madoc story note pre-Columbian references to Madoc were passed down through Welsh ballads and poems. Other experts contend Columbus researched Madoc's legend before setting sail on his own historic voyage. An Icelandic saga written in the twelfth century describes a "freeman from Wales" who sailed from the island of Lundy to the southern isles. Bards and poems about Madoc were shelved next to Leif Eriksson's adventures in libraries across Western Europe as early as 1250. However, these tales of Madoc ceased by 1282 when the Black Plague spread across Europe. Welsh poet Maredudd ap Rhys, who lived during the late fifteenth century, was the first to reference Madoc as a son of Owain Gwynedd, who voyaged to the sea.

Literature that traces Madoc and his role of integrating with native peoples in the New World dates back to 1583, when George Peckham wrote in *A True Report of the Late Discoveries of Newfound Landes* that the word *pengwyn* was Welsh in origin. *Pengwyn* translates to "white" (*gwyn*) "head" (*pen*). Equally fascinating to eighteenth-century Welsh immigrants was the fact that reports of Welsh-speaking Indian tribes proliferated throughout the interior of the United States. At one time it was speculated that at least fifteen tribes were descendants of Welsh Indians. The Madoc legend persevered until the nineteenth century, when writer Colonel Amos Stoddard opined that certain Welsh

Indian activities resembled lodges of freemasonry, which were distinctive of Druids and Wales.

Studies indicating a genetic link between modern Welsh and Native Americans were reported in 2007. Howard Kimberley, the founder of the Madoc International Research Association in Wales, attempted to prove genetically the presence of Madoc ancestors in both the Old World and New World and sought permission to test Native American bone samples that predate Columbus. Ken Lonewolf, a Pittsburgh engineer and Native American, heard about Kimberley's experiment and submitted his sample. Lonewolf was confident he descended from Welsh Indians, including a Shawnee leader named Chief White Madoc. DNA testing proved Kimberley and Lonewolf share the mitochondrial (female) DNA, but it's unclear when Lonewolf obtained his Welsh ancestry.

Other unanswered questions continue to puzzle historians. Remains of an ancient harbor were uncovered during excavations for a garden for a Rhos-on-Sea home. This North Wales seaport is where Madoc and his brother Riryd were to have set sail on his second voyage. On the other side of the Atlantic, stone fortifications at Fort Mountain in Georgia, Lookout Mountain in Alabama, and Old Stone Fort in Tennessee, were built before Columbus arrived in the Americas. Could these have been built by Madoc's second voyage of shipmates who were never found on his subsequent trip?

Evidence, or lack of it, renders the Madoc story more legend than fact. It is hardly ironic that the proliferation of

Madoc and his exploits took hold in the sixteenth century, at a time when England was competing with Spain in exploration of the New World. Humphrey Llwyd's *Cronica Walliae* (1559) chronicled Madoc's voyage to America, followed by George Peckham's *A True Report of the Late Discoveries of the Newfound Landes* (1583), David Powel's *The Historie of Cambria* (1584), and Richard Hakluyt's *The Principal Navigations, Voyages, Traffiques and Discoveries of the English Nation* (1598). These renditions highlighted English conquests used to squelch English embarrassment over the discovery of the Americas by Spain's Columbus. Some also believed the Madoc tale was created by Welsh-born King Henry VII to override Spain's claim to the New World. Yet other historians believe Madoc ap Meurig of the sixth century, not Madoc ap Gwynedd of the twelfth century, may have been the Madoc who really discovered America.

If political posturing by England was not enough to discredit the Madoc legend, the failure of the linguistic argument to hold water may put the proverbial nail in the coffin. Evidence suggests that the linguists who boasted of Indian language integration with Welsh words had virtually no knowledge of Welsh. In fact many purported Indian "Welsh" words are semantically related to other Siouan languages. Near the end of the eighteenth century, Welshman and Madoc believer John Evans came to the United States to investigate Welsh Indians. Starting on the East Coast, he ventured where any rumors of Welsh-speaking Indians took him. He wintered with the Mandan in 1796 and 1797 and told his British sponsors that there was no such thing as Welsh Indians. Experts believe that the members of the Lewis and Clark Expedition (1803–1806) also sought proof of the Mandan's Welsh origins, but after spending the winter of 1804–1805 with Mandan Indians, they decided Welsh Indians to be nonexistent. Genetically, the Welsh are not blond haired, blue eyed, and light skinned; they are predominately dark haired and dark eyed. Even if fair-skinned Welsh had settled in the New World, five centuries of intermarrying Native Americans would have rendered descendants with the dominant genes of dark skin, dark hair, and dark eyes.

Archeological ties to Madoc also have proven suspect. Archeologists hypothesize the Georgia, Alabama, and Tennessee fortifications were built preceding 1170, possibly six hundred to twelve hundred years earlier, most likely by Indians. Even second-century Roman coins found around the ruins seem unusual for twelfth-century Welshmen to be carrying. Archeologists purport that it is more probable the coins were collector's items recklessly lost. Historians point out that Rhos-on-Sea, where Madoc and Riryd were to have set sail, was far too shallow to accommodate a ship that was big enough to cross the Atlantic and hold up to 120 individuals.

So what became of Madoc and Welsh presence in the Ohio Valley? E. T. Cox's account of Devil's Backbone was rendered the most authoritative until archeologist Gerard Fowke visited the site. In 1902 Fowke admonished Cox by writing that Devil's

Backbone's stone fort was "only the natural outcrop of the heavy, evenly-bedded limestone . . . even a cook or mule-driver could have never made such a ridiculous blunder." The construction of the Big Four Railroad Bridge between 1888 and 1895 dealt a deathblow to the stone façade of Devil's Backbone. Subsequently, Rose Island amusement park was developed on the same location in 1920, further erasing any archeological evidence.

Other archeological finds have been lost over time, as well. The brass-plated armor engraved with a harp and mermaid found by John Brady disappeared over the course of time. In addition, the Roman coins found at the bridge construction site were eventually lost. Myth proponents hypothesize that nine-hundred-year-old coins can be easily bought in antique stores and haphazardly lost. Finally, with the purported loss of the gravestone allegedly dated 1186, any archaeological evidence to Madoc and his Welshmen no longer exists.

Whether fact or fiction, the story of Madoc and his Welshmen contributes to the rich Welsh oral history transcending both Old and New Worlds, highlights the challenges and inter-relationships settlers experienced in the New World, and continues to challenge historians seeking the truth about Madoc's conquests.

CHAPTER 2

The Search for Jonathan Swift's Silver Mines

For more than 250 years, treasure hunters have been fascinated by the legend of lost silver mines in eastern Kentucky. Whether the mines ever existed may be fact or folklore, but the lure of the discovery of the legendary Jonathan Swift silver mines has driven some to complete distraction.

William Forwood left Louisville to try to find the mysterious silver cache in Wolfe County, Kentucky, in 1851. Forwood's son gave him Swift's supposed journal and told his father, "You can take this, and if you find that mine, it is a fortune for you and for me and all others concerned." Although five years of searching turned up nothing, Forwood encouraged his son and grandson to search for the purported fortune. Three generations of the family tried to find the fortune before eventually abandoning their efforts.

A moderately wealthy couple now known only by the last name of Timmons, who met the elder Forwood in Louisville, was charmed by the potential fortune disclosed in the journal. Lured by the prospect of a quick fortune, the Timmonses uprooted their family and settled down in an eastern Kentucky cliff country village in hopes of finding the Swift riches. For thirty years the couple vigilantly prospected the area and even hired guides to canvass the area mentioned in Swift's journal. After Mr. Timmons died, Mrs. Timmons continued to press forward with her mission to find the silver. When she traveled back East to seek investors and hire help, she met a New York venture capitalist and fellow miner, S. A. Hazelton, who joined her in her efforts.

Although Mrs. Timmons ran out of money, her confidence was not shaken. She spent her last remaining years in a one-room hut with her sole possession: Swift's journal. Before she finally passed away, she asked a neighbor farmer to take a large package to the local post office. Addressed to a doctor in St. Louis, the package contained Swift's journal. Undeterred even by her own mortality, Mrs. Timmons sent the book to a benefactor with the hopes that someone would find the silver cache.

Having studied the journal in Mrs. Timmons's possession many times, Hazelton continued the search for another fifteen years. Each day he hoped would be the day his luck turned on the hidden wealth. He often confided to his local guide that he had found the exact location for sinking a shaft to strike the silver ore, but each time he would turn up nothing.

The prospect of finding silver in eastern Kentucky dates back to the arrival of Hernando De Soto. While venturing into the eastern region of Kentucky and Tennessee around 1540, the Cherokee Indians told De Soto of silver mines that surrounded the Appalachian Mountains. As they traveled toward the Mississippi River, De Soto's Spanish expedition supposedly detailed Indian metallurgy information during their quest for gold, colonies, and other evidence of prosperity. After the Spanish retreated in the seventeenth century, the French eventually came into the area. Both the French and Cherokee enslaved the Shawnee Indians and pressed them to work the mines and extract the precious ore.

As the French and Indian Wars ravaged the area, the Cherokee were waging another battle with the Shawnee over control of the silver mines. It was widely rumored that in the three hundred years since the discovery of the mines, millions of dollars' worth of silver were extracted. Even frontiersmen Daniel Boone and Christopher Gist noted observations about the silver rumored to be mined in the area.

These accounts eventually made their way to Jonathan Swift. Little is known about Swift's background. Swift is reported to have sailed from England to present-day America around 1750. He was a well-educated sailor who sought respite in North America after being suspected of piracy and other crimes and facing possible execution. He spent several years fur trading with the Shawnees in the Ohio Valley, eventually marrying the daughter of a chief. While trading with the Indians, he was captured by the French, but he escaped to Virginia.

Swift served in the armies of both General Edward Braddock and General George Washington during the French and Indian War. He befriended several North Carolina men (James Ireland, Samuel Blackburn, Isaac Campbell, Abram Flint, Harmon Staley, and Shadrach Jefferson) during Braddock's campaign to seize Fort Duquesne. Eventually mustered out of the British army, Swift made his way to Alexandria, Virginia. At one time, he was arrested in North Carolina as a counterfeiter. During the trial, he submitted as evidence a coin that was deemed pure silver, and all charges were eventually dropped.

While living in Alexandria contemplating his next move, Swift met a Frenchman, George Mundy. Mundy's tales of adventure piqued Swift's curiosity. Mundy claimed that, as a youth, he accompanied trappers traversing the virgin woodlands of Wolfe County, Kentucky. One of the trappers shot a bear and followed the wounded animal into a hole in a rock wall along the mountainside. Mundy's job was to go into the hole and bind the animal's legs so he could be dragged out. As Mundy crept through the small opening, he discovered an abandoned mine. He traveled farther along the shaft, stupefied by the wall of glistening silver that radiated from his torch light.

Mundy made his way back out and excitedly told the trappers of his find. The men began a futile effort to extract what silver they could. Their efforts did not go unnoticed: Shawnees had been surveying the party from the ridge tops. One morning, as the trapping party loaded their sacks of silver ore onto their horses, the Shawnee attacked them. All of the trappers were killed except Mundy, who had hid in the mine during the fighting. Eventually discovered, Mundy was enslaved by the Shawnee and pressed to prospect Indian mines that dotted the Red River Gorge. The Cherokee eventually raided one of the Shawnee camps where Mundy resided, took Mundy as one of their slaves, and used his talent to continue the excavation of former Shawnee mines that the Cherokees had appropriated. Mundy learned the history of the mines along the Red River Gorge area from Spanish visitors who had befriended the Cherokees.

The French, who arrived shortly after the Spanish left the area to sell their largesse, also befriended the Cherokee. This alliance proved advantageous not only for the Cherokee mining operations, but also for thwarting the westward expansion of British and American colonies. The amount of silver excavated from the area was purported to have financed the French army during the French and Indian War. Years later, human bones, European horn buttons, and even makeshift furnace walls were discovered in rock cavities throughout the Appalachian Mountains, offering evidence that Spanish and French forces had been present in the southeastern Cumberland region.

In 1754 British General Edward Braddock was sent to Kentucky to fight the French and their Cherokee allies. Mundy, the Cherokee slave, fought alongside the French but was eventually captured by the British. After being taken to Alexandria for questioning, Mundy was released. Mundy had no place to go and eventually wandered the streets begging for food or money. He soon met Jonathan Swift, who felt sorry for the young man and took him under his wing. Grateful to Swift, Mundy relayed his adventures and tales of the abandoned silver mines that lay undisturbed in Kentucky's wilderness. Swift was probably already familiar with tales of silver mines from his own fur trading experiences with the Indians, but Mundy's accounts may have encouraged him to press forward with his own exploration.

Swift began to get his expedition ready. After heading to Cuba to secure financing, Swift hired several men, including skilled miners and former British soldiers whom he had fought alongside. In late spring of 1760, Swift, Mundy, and their entourage headed for the foothills of Kentucky's Appalachian Mountains. Swift carried a journal and recorded his travels, opening with their arrival in Floyd County. It took Mundy a while to become reacclimated to the area and points of reference, but eventually the party arrived at a myrtle thicket Mundy noted as near one of the mine entrances. From there Mundy followed a familiar path that shortly led the group to the mine. The party made a primitive furnace for smelting ore and began excavation. Of the silver they found, the men shaped the pieces into ingots, or small bars, that could be easily transported in their horse satchels. Swift suggested the party halt further digging, take their largesse back to Alexandria, and make plans for another expedition.

As they began their second expedition, Swift and his men set out to seek their fortune by way of Bell County. According

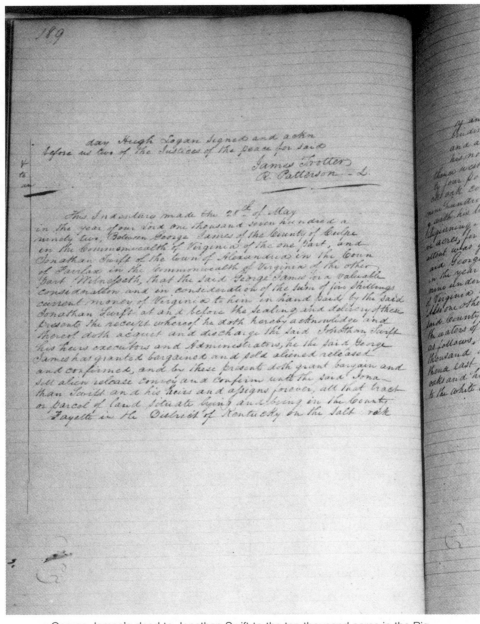

George James's deed to Jonathan Swift to the ten thousand acres in the Big Sandy region of Kentucky, where the silver "mine" was located.

to Swift's journal, the fortune they had struck a year earlier was a tease compared to the amount of silver they pulled out of the Bell County mine. Swift and his crew spent seven months mining the ore and converting it to ingots. Swift arrived in Alexandria in December 1760 with enough accumulated wealth to team up with a former coin engraver from the Royal Mint of England— Seth Montgomery—and begin a trading company and purchase two ships. Records confirm that Swift and Montgomery were insured by Lloyd's Registry from 1761 to 1767 as sea captains.

Having secured funds from their venture, Swift and Montgomery set out on another mining expedition on June 5, 1761. When the group reached the fork heads of the Sandy River, they divided into two smaller parties. Mundy traveled west to locate new mines, while Swift traveled to the mine he had previously excavated. Montgomery then set to work on making counterfeit British crowns from the ingots. Swift and Montgomery left the party in December 1761 and headed to Alexandria with the intention of purchasing two more ships to transport their silver coins, along with fur and other goods, back to England. Swift's companions maintained the operation was such an efficient clandestine venture that barrels of illegal coins reportedly infiltrated both England and the American colonies each time the Swift party returned from an expedition.

Swift and Montgomery began their third trip in March 1762 by way of Fort Pitt. Up until this time their operations had been relatively unhampered. However, the men discovered Indian skirmishes were jeopardizing safety, so Swift and Montgomery decided to secure a larger party of well-armed men for protection. Two horses drowned while the group was crossing the Kanawha River. When Swift's party reached the fork in the Big Sandy River, the group cast lots to see which members of the party would have to mine. By the time Swift's party reached the location where he had left his workers in the winter of 1761, Swift discovered the men had disappeared. Regardless, Swift's party continued excavation operations for both old and new mines during the remainder of 1762 and all the way through 1764.

The French and Indian War failed to thwart trips back and forth to the mines. In April 1765 the miners left Mundy's house along the New River, reaching lower mines by May. Although the previous year had not been profitable, the year 1765 proved to be a bountiful time. The group mined so much silver they were unable to carry all of it home, and they buried the remaining silver in a secret cave. However, party scuffles and fear of discovery began to escalate. At Christmastime in 1765, two men in the party, Fletcher and Flint, got drunk and wounded each other in a duel. Flint buried 240,000 British crowns, and Fletcher hid 460,000 near Mundy's house along the New River in North Carolina. Fletcher passed away seven months later. In late fall of 1768, the party was ambushed while returning from a mine; two men were killed, and another was wounded. Some men in the party feared they would be cheated from their money in North Carolina and suspended operations in that state.

The last expedition began in May 1769 from Mundy's house along the New River and Cumberland Gap. The pack train had grown so large that it was slow and unyielding. However, the party eventually made it to the lower mines in June and worked until October. The men had determined they had enough wealth to get through the next three years. Men were paid more than seven times their wages, and the remaining bounty was sealed in a great Shawnee cavern. During that time, Swift headed for England to amass more funds and materials for a full-scale operation. After the party returned to Virginia by way of the Big Sandy River and Fort Pitt, Swift wrote in his journal:

> We left between $22,000 and $30,000 and crowns on a large creek, running near a south course. Close to the spot we marked our names (Swift, Jefferson, Mundy, and others) on a beech tree, with a compass square and trowel. No great distance from this place we left $15,000 of the same kin, marking three or four trees with marks. Not far from these we left the prize, near a forked white oak, and three feet underground, and laid two long stones across it, marking several stones close about it. At the forks of Sandy, close by the fork, is a small rock, having a spring in one end of it. Between it and a small branch we hid a prize under the ground; it was valued at $6,000. We likewise left $3,000 buried in the rock of the rock house.

On December 11, 1769, all operations ceased in Alexandria, Virginia, as Swift sailed to England to attract investors and more miners for larger scale operations. Instead of expanding his business, however, Swift spent the next fifteen years in jail for disputing British colonial policies. By the time he was released from prison, he was nearly blind. He sailed back to America to reconnect with his associates, but he found many were unaccountable. Several of the men, including Mundy, attempted to return to the mines but were never heard from again. Undeterred, Swift reunited with a former partner named McClintrock. After assembling a party of two Frenchmen and several Indians, they left Alexandria in 1790. Swift told the party that once they found the hidden bounty, the money would be used to mount larger mining operations. Although Swift believed he was following old trails, his eyesight failed to help him locate key landmarks. Moreover, the last successful expedition had taken great pains to effectively seal their bounty from fortune hunters, making the treasures even more difficult to find.

The itinerant party spent several weeks trekking the area, but they found nothing. They finally abandoned their efforts when provisions ran low. Swift lived out his remaining years alone and blind, passing away in 1800.

And what about his journal? Swift distrusted some of the men in his last expedition, so he left the journal in the possession of a widower, Mrs. Renfro, whom Swift wanted to marry. Interestingly, Mrs. Renfro's late husband had bequeathed to her a large tract of land.

The mystery of the Swift silver mines remains as elusive as its namesake. Details about Jonathan Swift's background remain sketchy. Historical records indicate that a merchant named Jonathan Swift lived in Alexandria, Virginia. However, research has determined that this merchant Swift acquired and redeeded land in 1809—nine years after records show that a certain blind man named Swift had died. In addition, the merchant Swift was born in Milton, Massachusetts, moved to Alexandria in 1785, and became a prominent citizen in Virginia before dying in 1824.

Some hypothesize that the legend is a ruse for a land scheme or counterfeiting operation. One of the first individuals to reference Swift's mine after 1800 was John Filson, who was also the first person to write about and map Kentucky. Filson wrote about land and traveled extensively throughout the state, even recording he had discovered the mine. Some have posited that the tale was possibly a scheme to lure colonists west. Still others believe the tale was a cover for an illegal counterfeit coin operation between mainland Europe and America. And some speculate Swift was actually a Spanish buccaneer who profited from a thriving piracy ring in the Atlantic.

Although most geologists concur that silver may be found in the sandstones of Kentucky, it is highly unlikely that the ore could be found in vast quantities. They also agree that western and central Kentucky harbor more silver ore than eastern Kentucky. Moreover, strip mining and highway transportation projects in eastern Kentucky during the last century should have unveiled any notable quantities of silver.

Based on the geographical descriptions Swift provided in his journal, the Appalachian breaks and headwaters hugging the Kentucky-Tennessee border seem to be the most likely area where he would buried his treasure. But as the legend has aged, the paths and landmarks have changed, and variations of the tale have multiplied as they've been passed down from early settlers to their modern descendants.

One theory even suggests that Swift may have discovered a material that only looked like silver. In 1854 a geology professor examined the ore from the purported Bell County Swift mine. It contained lead sulfide (galena), a material that could be easily mistaken for silver. Could Swift and his men have mistaken this material for genuine silver?

Even Swift's journal reportedly has been reproduced in as many as thirty-six versions. Swift apparently kept a copy of his journal with him so that he could share—or possibly sell—its contents to whomever he pleased. However, landmarks, paths, and even the supporting cast of characters would change with each edition. Without an original journal available, it is difficult for historians to investigate evidence to confirm an authoritative version.

Another theory contends Mundy was actually a North Carolina soldier named Jonathan Munday who fought alongside Swift in Braddock's army. In yet another version, Swift is taken to a mine by Mundy or Monde (a Frenchmen), but driven from the mine in an Indian attack. As the story goes, Swift later killed Mundy out of fear he would disclose the location.

One of most celebrated versions of Swift's journal contains references to freemasonry. The Freemasons were a fraternal organization in eighteenth-century Europe, and the group's popularity spread to the American colonies. Freemasonry has prominent symbols often used in stonemasonry, including a compass (compass square and trowel on a tree), a stone (Swift's rock landmarks), and certain numbers (three feet underground; $3,000), among others. Even if Swift existed, no evidence concludes that he was a Freemason. However, it is possible that the writer of one version may have had freemasonry connections.

No matter what evidence or lack of evidence conjures up, the Swift silver mines legend is pervasive in eastern Kentucky, Tennessee, Virginia, and North Carolina. Campton, Kentucky, hosts a Swift Silver Mine Festival every Labor Day weekend. The event has hosted up to twelve thousand people and is marked with a parade along Campton's Main Street. The most popular activity capping the three-day weekend is a competitive metal detector hunt, and the entire festival continues to uphold the enduring Kentucky legend of Jonathan Swift's lost silver mines.

CHAPTER 3

Who Really Invented Bourbon Whiskey?

Kentucky is home to 98 percent of the country's bourbon distilleries, making the Bluegrass State synonymous with Kentucky bourbon. But the inventor of the state's most famous product is far more difficult to determine.

Historical accounts dating back to the mid-eighteenth century reveal the identity of several early distillers in Kentucky, including Elijah Craig, who built a distillery in Louisville in 1789. Although Craig has long been heralded as the father of bourbon whiskey, he probably was not the first person to distill the liquor. In fact he may have earned the title after an accident that forever changed the flavor and color of corn whiskey.

As the story goes, a fire broke out in Craig's distillery and burned many of his barrel staves. Instead of throwing out the barrels, Craig turned the charred staves to the inside of the containers, filled them with his corn whiskey, and shipped them downriver to New Orleans. During the slow journey, the whiskey seeped beneath the charred layers of the barrels, interacted with the caramelized wood, and aged with an amber glow. By the time the shipment arrived in New Orleans, the whiskey had mellowed so much that it had an extraordinarily sweet, smooth flavor.

Craig may not have even been the first to age whiskey with charred oak barrels. Another version of the story states that a thrifty distiller wanted to store his liquor in barrels previously used for shipping fish. To get rid of the fish smell, he scorched the inside of the barrels. After tasting the liquor in the charred barrels, he discovered a smoother flavor and richer color. A third account contends a cooper accidentally scorched the barrel staves. When the customer tasted the whiskey, he was so enthralled by the taste that he asked for more stock from the same barrels.

Although there is little doubt that Elijah Craig was a distiller, christening him as the father of bourbon whiskey may be a long shot. Craig was born in Orange County, Virginia, in 1743, one of the sons of Mary "Polly" Craig, a heroine of Bryan Station. Elijah converted to the Baptist faith along with his brothers Lewis and Joseph, and he became an ordained minister by 1771. But Elijah ran into the law early on, serving time in jail with Lewis in Virginia for preaching without a license from the Anglican Church. He was later jailed for writing blasphemous pamphlets, as well as preaching vitriolic sermons that weighed heavily against the Anglican Church.

Seeking refuge from religious persecution, Elijah traveled to present-day Scott County and cofounded the Great (Buffalo) Crossing Church with both brothers by 1785. Elijah also purchased one thousand acres and eventually plotted the town of Georgetown. He took advantage of the nearby North Elkhorn Creek by erecting Georgetown's earliest dam, and he was responsible for developing a number of "firsts" in Kentucky: the state's first paper factory, grist mill, ropewalk, and fulling mill for woolens. But his entrepreneurial spirit may have been equal only to his passion in the pulpit. In addition to becoming known for his business acumen, Elijah extended his notoriety by actively preaching in as many as four churches in the community. He also established and administered Rittenhouse Academy, the first classical school in the state, in 1787. Eventually acquiring more than four thousand acres, he donated some of the land for the establishment of Georgetown College, the first Baptist college founded west of the Allegheny Mountains.

Though historical records prove that Elijah Craig was a distiller, did he distill the state's first bourbon whiskey? Evidence remains inconclusive. Early Kentucky historians acknowledged Craig's paper mills, but failed to acknowledge his bourbon whiskey distillery. Moreover, he was sued by the government for failing to pay taxes on his whiskey and eventually paid $140 excise taxes on September 26, 1790. Some surmise that the evangelical Elijah Craig was the perfect ruse manufactured by distillers to undermine Prohibitionists during the late 1800s.

The conflict between religion and intemperance was not an issue for eighteenth-century pioneers like Craig. No records discredit frontier religious figures from drinking or making liquor. In fact, distilling liquor was an outgrowth of farming, if not a cultural way of life for frontiersmen. Farmers reverted to corn liquor production when they had a corn surplus. And most pioneers were appreciative of corn whiskey, since it was often used for medicinal purposes, such as treating colds, toothaches, rheumatism, and snakebites, and as a disinfectant for cuts and bruises.

Distillers like Craig found that the geography and temperatures in Kentucky made it a natural venue for distilling, a mechanical process of heat, condensation, and vaporization. Bourbon whiskey is comprised of a grain mixture of malted barley, wheat, rye, and more than 51 percent corn. The varying ratios of corn, barley, wheat, and rye distinguish corn, Scotch malt, rye, bourbon, and Tennessee whiskey from each other.

Using a water- or horse-powered grist mill, early distillers mixed ground corn with rye meal and calcium-rich limestone water to form a "mash bill." Corn gives whiskey strength and body. The mixture was scalded and combined with any mash bill, or "slop," from earlier distillations, producing a thick pudding. This was known as sour mash; sweet mash used fresh yeast for every new batch. The mash was allowed to cool for one day, known as a souring period, before it was stirred and broken up. Then barley malt was added. This process converted the grain starch to soluble sugar. After cycles of heating and cooling, the mash was broken up by a mashing oar and poured into an open-topped fermenting still. Yeast was then added and fermented with the limestone water to a liquid "wash" or "distiller's beer." The wash remained in the still between seventy-two and ninety-six hours at a temperature of seventy-five degrees.

During Elijah Craig's time, a fermenting still was comprised of two parts: A round copper kettle with a bulbous top sat over an open flame within a brick furnace. A tapered neck connected the kettle to a condenser of spiral tubing (or "worm"), which was immersed in a trough or tub of circulating cold water. Most distilleries were located near a creek or spring because the water for distilling should be colder than 56 degrees to condense the steam. Ideally, cold limestone water flowed into the worm and mixed with the fermented wash vaporized by the cold water. The wash was then distilled to 65 to 80 percent alcohol using a pot still. Since alcohol evaporates at a lower temperature than water—alcohol boils at 173 degrees and water boils at 212 degrees—timing was crucial. A lid fastened to the still at the peak boiling point allowed the alcohol to evaporate and condense.

The first vapor, called a foreshot, containing a mix of solid matter, alcohol, and water, passed through the worm. After a while more water boiled, and then the largest amount of potable alcohol flowed through the worm. The art to distilling narrowed down to drawing off the most potable alcohol and as little water as possible. The clear alcohol was then placed in barrels, preferably charred oak, which allowed oxidation to occur and changed the spirit to a caramel color. Then sugar was added to mellow the flavor.

With these stills it could take one day to make ten gallons of bourbon whiskey; therefore two barrels took one week to produce. Rotating barrels helped the aging process. However, unlike wine, the longer bourbon whiskey ages, the more is lost to evaporation and the outside environment. In a twelve-year-old bourbon whiskey, for instance, as much as 40 percent could have been lost to evaporation.

A distillery was an economic boost to the local community. It provided a market not only for local grain and barley, but also for local cordwood to cook the grain and barley into fermented mash. Consistent with pioneer life, very little of the ingredients used in whiskey making were wasted. The portion of the fermented mash that remained after distillation was used for animal feed. Cooperages, or barrel manufacturers, used the barrel staves. Growth in the distilling industry required men, called teamsters, to actually transport the whiskey to market. The slow, lengthy trips for transporting the heavy barrels by wagon or boat exacted ideal conditions for aging bourbon whiskey.

If Elijah Craig was not the first bourbon whiskey distiller, who was? The answer may never be truly known. Even finding evidence for an exact date in which bourbon whiskey was first distilled is difficult to pinpoint. The earliest evidence of Kentucky distilling dates back to 1776. Around that time, Elijah

Making "Moonshine" in Kentucky. (Printed verso reads: "Back in the hills, off the beaten highway, the mountaineers have their own distilleries, making powerful moonshine called 'Mountain Dew.'") (1943)

Pepper relocated from Virginia to Frankfort Pike, near Lexington, and built a log cabin distillery. He sold a product named "Old 1776" and advertised it with the slogan "Born with the Republic." Family members ran the business until 1906, when the distillery and its brand were sold.

Still others have been named as the possible first master distiller. John Ritchie is purported to have built a still outside of Bardstown in 1777, while Henry Hudson Wathen began a still in 1787 near Lebanon. Wathen descendants ran the family distillery through the twentieth century, until the business was sold to the parent company of Jim Beam. Ironically, descendants of Jacob Beam purportedly have evidence that the first Beam started distilling in 1787. More evidence leans to David Stewart, who placed a June 1789 ad offering "a copper still of 120 gallons capacity, with a good copper and pewter worm."

Liquor and the law seem to have collided even for the first distillers. Evan Williams is credited as the first commercial distiller, beginning in Louisville in 1783. After being indicted for making whiskey without a license, he turned the tables and was elected to Louisville's first Board of Trustees in 1797. During his tenure the board enacted a rule stipulating that any "ardent or spirituous liquors brought to meetings would be forfeited for the use of the Board after adjournment." Another distiller, Jacob Myers, operated a still in Lincoln County. During his 1781 run for election to the Virginia House of Burgesses, Myers attempted to use whiskey to buy votes over his opponent, Benjamin Logan, the famed Indian fighter who served under George Rogers Clark. Myers lost the election.

Still others contend James Garrard, another Baptist preacher, may have been the patriarch of American bourbon. Garrard was indicted in 1787 by a Bourbon County grand jury for selling liquor without a license. In an interesting turn of events, the minister was later ejected by his own church but became a high-ranking politician, shaping Kentucky's state constitution and governing the state for two terms.

Bourbon whiskey traces its roots to French, German, and Scotch-Irish cultures. It is because of this history that many believe the first bourbon distillers may have actually been

French. French distillers, especially in New Orleans, served an early market for charred oak barrel–aged whiskey, since the spirit resembled cognac in its distillery production. In fact some historians credit French brothers John and Louis Tarascon as the first bourbon distillers. The Tarascon brothers immigrated to the United States at the onset of the French Revolution in 1789. The brothers founded a warehouse and mill at Shipping-port at the Falls of the Ohio to expedite trade between Louisville and New Orleans. Researchers postulate that the brothers bought the whiskey and transferred it into charred barrels for transporting to residents of New Orleans who sought cognac rather than whiskey. The Tarascon brothers came from an area of France that was near the Cognac region. However, most Scotch-Irish were familiar with protecting the quality of the spirit in the aging process, so the likelihood of a Scotsman or Irishman being the first distiller is plausible as well.

If the first distiller is difficult to pinpoint, so too is the exact location of the first distillery. Before 1776, all of Kentucky was part of Fincastle County, Virginia. By 1780 Jefferson, Lincoln, and Fayette Counties were spun off from this expansive tract of land. The Virginia legislature had further sliced up Fayette County into nine counties by the time Kentucky reached state-hood in 1792. Bourbon County, which covered a substantial part of the north-central part of the state, derived from the northern tip of Fayette County. Bourbon County was not named for its production of whiskey, but for a French royal family in appreciation for French aid during the American Revolution. Bourbon County eventually segregated into thirty-three counties, an action further muddying the waters for the location of the first distillery. Ironically, no bourbon is currently produced in Bourbon County, Kentucky.

The first public record using the term *bourbon* to describe whiskey comes from the *Western Citizen* newspaper published in Paris, Kentucky in 1821. Place names were used for spirits in order to identify the region from which the liquor originated. For example, bourbon whiskey is named to differentiate itself from Monongahela rye, a Pennsylvania whiskey. But no matter what its origin, bourbon whiskey is and will forever be synonymous with Kentucky.

CHAPTER 4

Secrets of the Old Talbott Tavern

For more than two hundred years, the Old Talbott Tavern has welcomed visitors to Court Square in the heart of Bardstown, Kentucky. Known as the oldest Western stagecoach stop still in business today, the stone building was constructed in 1779 as a stop for weary travelers along the rugged frontier trail. But local residents, overnight guests, and tavern employees insist that several of those visitors from long ago have never left the building.

Located at the crossroads of major stagecoach routes, the tavern was a popular stop for hundreds of individuals venturing to the western frontier. The Old Talbott Tavern opened for business shortly before settlers established Bardstown, the second-oldest city in Kentucky, in 1780.

One of the first maps of Bardstown reveals that the site of the Old Talbott Tavern was originally purchased by a gentleman named Hynes, and a stone building constructed on the property was known as the Hynes Hotel. Although the identity of the

Old Talbott Tavern in Bardstown, Kentucky

PHOTO COURTESY OF THE UNIVERSITY OF KENTUCKY

stonemason is unknown, architectural experts say the Old Talbott Tavern is a rare example of Flemish bond stonework.

Through the years the stone building was known by various names, such as the Newman House, Bardstown Hotel, and the Old Stone Tavern. The Talbott Tavern became the official name around 1885, when George Talbott purchased the business.

The Talbott Tavern served not only as a business, but also as a home for Talbott, his wife, and their twelve children. Life on the frontier, however, brought hardships and heartache for the family. During one winter four of the children passed away. Another child died from a fall down the stairs, and the oldest daughter hanged herself, distraught over a tumultuous love affair. After Talbott took his last breath at the inn in 1912, his widow Annie changed the name of the business to the Talbott Hotel.

Only a few families have owned the Old Talbott Tavern since its construction in the 1770s, and several owners were connected directly to bourbon distilleries in the area. T. D. Beam, brother of Jim Beam, purchased the Old Talbott Tavern from Annie Talbott in 1916, and he operated the business until selling the establishment in 1926 to the Tom Moore family, who also operated a local bourbon distillery. Other owners and associates of competing bourbon distilleries in the area, such as Maker's Mark and Heaven Hill Distillery, were frequent patrons of the tavern.

Numerous historical figures crossed the threshold of the Old Talbott Tavern over the years, seeking food, drink, and shelter during their journeys. One of the earliest and most famous visitors was Daniel Boone, who was subpoenaed to give a deposition at the stone tavern on the court square in April 1792. At the time, the courthouse was still under construction. Another illustrious visitor was General George Rogers Clark, who used the tavern as a base during the end of the Revolutionary War. And folklore claims nine-year-old Abraham Lincoln stayed at the tavern as he traveled through Kentucky with his parents.

In the 1830s a group of volunteers known as the Bardstown Mustangs held regular meetings at the tavern. The group fought in the war of Texas independence, and only one member of the group survived the massacre at Goliad in October 1835. Another historical figure associated with the tavern was Alexander Walters, whose mother was a tavern cook. Walters was born in the pantry of the Old Talbott Tavern in 1858. Years later he led a group known as the National Negro Committee, which eventually became the National Association for the Advancement of Colored People. And during the Civil War in 1862, Confederate troops took over the tavern for two weeks, using it as a staging area for the bloody battle of Perryville.

Some researchers say author Washington Irving was inspired to write his short story "Stolen Kiss" while dining at the tavern. The inspiration stemmed from observing a gentleman steal a kiss from a young lady during lunch. Renowned artist John James Audubon dined at the tavern as well.

Prominent figures continued to frequent the Old Talbott Tavern throughout the twentieth century, like food critic Duncan Hines, who wrote a favorable review of his meal at the tavern. General George S. Patton visited the tavern so often that management placed a brass nameplate on Patton's favorite table. And newspaper accounts reveal that cowboy Roy Rogers even stayed overnight and had breakfast at the Talbott during a horse-buying trip to Kentucky in 1945.

Undoubtedly the Old Talbott Tavern has witnessed more than two centuries of history and played a significant role in the history of the Western frontier. Today the old stone structure vibrates with remembrances—and perhaps spirits—of the past. Employees claim that unexplainable events like lanterns suddenly lighting up, chairs being moved across a room, and lost objects turning up in odd places continue to occur on a frequent basis.

Well into the twenty-first century, several employees of the Old Talbott Tavern were closing the business for the night when they saw the figure of a man wearing a long coat. Assuming everyone had left the building for the evening, the women became alarmed as they watched the man walk across the landing of the stairs on the second floor.

The employees scurried up the stairs to investigate. They reached the second floor just as the man disappeared through the fire escape door. Close on his heels, the tavern manager rushed down the hall, hurled open the door, and found herself face-to-face with the stranger standing on the landing. Throwing back his head, he laughed out loud. Then he suddenly disappeared.

Sometime later one of those tavern employees saw a familiar face pop up on the screen of her television during a program about famed outlaw Jesse James. As she examined the photograph in front of her, she suddenly realized the man in that picture was the same man she had encountered on the fire escape landing.

According to local lore, the notorious James actually stayed at the Old Talbott Tavern on several occasions while visiting relatives in the area. His mother was born only a few miles from Bardstown, and his cousin Donnie Pence served as the sheriff of Nelson County, Kentucky, for thirty years.

On one visit James stayed in one of the rooms on the second floor, located in a portion of the building that had been added to the original structure in the 1790s. Murals painted on one wall of the room featured scenes of Don Quixote, a volcano, and tropical trees. Popular legend contends that exiled French King Louis-Philippe painted the scenes during a visit to Bardstown in 1797. The owners of the Old Talbott Tavern rediscovered the murals in 1926 as they redecorated and stripped wallpaper from the room.

As the story goes, James may have enjoyed far too much of the sweet taste of local bourbon in the tavern before retiring for the evening. Awakening in the middle of the night, James thought he saw birds flying out of the murals in his room. True to form, the outlaw grabbed his gun and shot a round of bullets at the imaginary feathered creatures. Today three bullet holes remain in the wall of the room, visible proof of James's trigger-happy reputation.

In recent years guests in the dining room have been stunned to see objects moving on their tables. Diners have reported that silverware balanced on the rim of a bowl has rocked back and forth and plates have slid across the table without explanation. One stunned guest even claimed that a glass of water rose from the table and landed in the middle of the floor without a single drop of water spilling from the glass.

Guests have frequently reported ghost sightings and eerie noises permeating throughout the building, especially in the spooky upstairs hallways. One guest, for instance, complained about the sounds of boisterous children laughing and running in and out of the room next door, but no other guests had been staying in the hotel that evening. Another guest claimed he awoke in the middle of the night, unable to move, as balls of light floated above the bed. As soon as the strange lights disappeared, his limbs began working again, allowing him to get out of bed.

Paranormal investigators using an electromagnetic field (EMF) meter have detected ghosts of children in the tavern. One of the main pieces of equipment used in ghost detection, EMF meters detect disturbances in the natural electromagnetic fields of their surroundings. Paranormal investigators consider these disturbances good indications of a ghostly presence. One tour group in the tavern witnessed the spirit of a little girl who answered questions by making the EMF meter lights go off and on. The ghostly lass even responded to requests to open the door and turn off the lights to the chandeliers. Staff members have referred to her as Annie, Becka, and several other names, but no one has been able to verify her identity. Could the ghost be the spirit of one of the Talbott children who died in the tavern? Or perhaps she is one of the Talbott daughters who decided not to leave her earthly home?

Several guests have insisted that an adult female ghost also resides in the Old Talbott Tavern. Overnight guests have reported being awakened by a lady in white standing by their bed. The terrified guests watched in silent horror as the ghostly form floated across the room and disappeared through the window.

The ghost of a lady with wavy brown hair, wearing a long white dress in the style of the early 1800s, has also been seen during the day in the dining room. Some suspect the ghost is the spirit of a woman who supposedly hung herself on a rope that dangled from a chandelier in the tavern. Though candles once lit the chandelier, the same light fixture now has electrical wiring and remains in use.

On occasion guests have reported seeing male ghosts in frontier-style clothing. But the most terrifying sight was a headless, spectral figure wearing black clothing with a brass or gold-tone covering over its chest. Visitors have encountered the phantom both upstairs and downstairs, in the hallways, the kitchen, and the basement.

Guests have also reported televisions in the rooms turning on and off throughout the night and excessively high temperatures awakening them from sleep. Even though the guests claim to have turned down the heat controls in their rooms, they were awakened again by the stifling heat. Numerous guests have also claimed to have heard knocks on the doors and finding no one in the hallway. Some guests have even heard someone playing an old piano and the sound of voices from empty areas.

In one written account of an overnight stay at the Old Talbott Tavern, a guest reported she felt as though someone was watching her as soon as she checked into her room. She even thought she saw a shadow move across the room and into the bathroom. As soon as she turned off the lights in the room to settle down for the night, noises erupted from every direction: doors slamming, water running, a man sneezing, and loud footsteps in the hall. The door to the room rattled and banged, as if someone had grabbed the doorknob and was trying to push open the door. Throughout the night she continued to hear different sounds, including eleven bell chimes at four o'clock in the morning, the clomp of horses' hooves on the street, a trio of men talking and laughing, and the stomp of footsteps throughout the inn. She finally inserted some cotton into her ears to drown out the noises. By the time she fell into a restless sleep, she dreamed about a hanging in the courtyard, which was located outside the window of her room. She later discovered the city jail had once been located next door to the tavern, and many hangings had taken place on the property.

With all the strange noises bellowing through the tavern, one former employee decided to see if she could catch any of the sounds on tape. One evening before leaving work, she set up recording equipment to capture any movement or sounds that might occur during the night. To complete her experiment, she returned to the tavern the next morning, retrieved the equipment, and took the recordings to a radio station for help in deciphering the taped noises. When the operators of the radio station ran the tapes on a slow speed, they could distinctly hear a female voice saying, "Welcome to the Talbott." The employee suspected the voice may have belonged to Annie Talbott, the widow of George Talbott.

In the early morning hours of March 7, 1998, a devastating fire swept through the second floor of the Old Talbott Tavern. The blaze destroyed the roof, antiques dating back to the 1800s, old tavern records and registration logs, and many original photos. The wall murals reportedly painted by the exiled King Louis-Philippe of France suffered heavy damage, although the three holes in the wall from the bullets shot by Jesse James still remain. The main floor suffered from smoke and water damage.

During renovations construction workers uncovered more unexplainable mysteries in the building, including a sub-basement, underground tunnels, and stairways leading to nowhere. By the time the Old Talbott Tavern reopened for business in November 1999, employees and guests were astonished to find that the ghostly activities had only intensified. Guests were even finding balls of light, known as orbs, in recent photographs taken at the site. To paranormal investigators, the orbs are believed to be life forces.

Fortunately employees of the Old Talbott Tavern claim that the spirits within the establishment are merely playful, noisy spirits who have never harmed anyone. But the increased frequency of ghostly manifestations since the fire has caught the attention of major cable networks. The Old Talbott Tavern has been featured in segments on the Food Network and the Travel Channel, and the business is ranked as the thirteenth most haunted inn in the United States.

Today visitors can step back in time as soon as they cross the threshold of the Old Talbott Tavern. The main tavern has been preserved with original, overhead log beams and two stone fireplaces that once provided warmth for guests. Though the original shelving and cabinet doors surrounding the fireplaces are warped and worn from age and the heat of the fireplaces, the setting emits an authentic charm of the early frontier. Thick, wide timbers cover the floor, and the creaking floorboards only emphasize the passage of time.

Diners can also enjoy Kentucky specialties in the same room where figures from history, such as Jesse James, General George Patton, and many more, once dined. To document the ghostly encounters that continue today, the Old Talbott Tavern provides journals in each room so guests can write about their experiences during their stay.

CHAPTER 5

What Caused Livestock to Tremble?

In the early part of the nineteenth century, many Kentucky farmers noticed their sheep were exhibiting odd behaviors, such as gritting their teeth and suddenly losing their appetite. Little did the farmers realize their herds were suffering from a mysterious illness that would baffle researchers for more than 150 years.

More symptoms quickly escalated within the herds. Over time the sheep's breathing became rapid, jerky, and labored. If driven only a few yards, they would stiffen their muscles and eventually suffer from muscle spasms and trembles. After the second or third day, the sheep became immobile. If they attempted to stand, severe trembling would overcome the animals. Eventually unable to rise from the ground, the sheep would lay comatose until death occurred.

But sheep were not the only animals afflicted by the mysterious condition. Hogs and cows suffered a similar fate. However, cows also experienced chronic constipation. Farmers and cattle traders could detect the disease only by running the herd for about twenty minutes to see if the animals would begin to tremble. Symptoms appeared prevalent during the spring and summer but rarely occurred in the winter months. Animals grazing in wooded, uncultivated small patches of land of about forty acres or less seemed to have a greater propensity for getting the trembles. However, not every animal that suffered from the puzzling condition died. Fatal cases of the "trembles" lasted no more than ten days, often before anyone could detect the illness or attempt to solve the problem.

Initially confined to the region surrounding Cincinnati, the disease began to spring up in Kentucky, Indiana, and farther points south and west. To make matters worse, the strange affliction began to strike humans, too. In the initial stage, victims experienced odd trembling and muscular pain generally located in the calf of the leg. A loss of appetite, constipation, and dehydration often continued for a week to ten days, until a victim recovered or advanced to the next stage.

Unceasing vomiting signaled the next stage, which could lead to seizures, coma, and sometimes death. Vomited material was marked by a dark bluish color and acetone smell. Victims exhibited flabby, sunken abdomens that lacked any intestinal contractions due to lack of appetite and constant vomiting. They also complained of a burning sensation in their stomachs and constant feelings of unquenchable thirst. Those afflicted never ran a high fever, and their skin felt cool to the touch. In some circumstances, patients could not tolerate the touch of fabric on their skin, except on the extremities.

The last and fatal stage was marked by a swollen tongue lined with a white film or "fur." Caregivers could easily identify patients who had the puzzling disease by the smell of their breath, which gave off a peculiar sweet, garlicky odor. The smell resembled the breath of diabetic patients before the use of insulin. Hiccups were not uncommon in the latter stage of the disease.

Treatment was comprised of early nineteenth-century pharmacology that was dispensed according to archaic medical advice. Dating back to ancient Greeks, bleeding less than a pint of blood and purging were two unsuccessful remedies. Tonics, wine, and salted meats offered mixed results. Alkaline lye was another treatment, but no one could determine if the patient suffered more harm from the treatment or the disease. Insects or mustard plaster applied to the stomach or ankles produced blisters in the hope of eliminating the disease through blood extraction. Enemas induced by calomel were another treatment, administered along with opium, to quiet the inflammation of the stomach.

No matter the treatment, patients who did not die quickly recovered slowly. Estimates of the mortality rate for individuals suffering from this unidentifiable illness ranged from 10 to 25 percent, although published accounts of the disease convinced people to believe there were many more victims. Relapses and protracted fatigue often disabled survivors. Chronic symptoms of appetite loss, flaring constipation, and fatigue became lifelong reminders of the disease.

Since adequately trained physicians were rare on the frontier, tracking and data documentation of disease survivors and victims were nonexistent and happenstance. Moreover, the medical community paid little attention to the epidemic. One of the few scientific publications to address the issue was the *Medical Repository,* America's first medical journal, which started in New York in 1797. In 1812, the publication reprinted a front-page article from the *Cincinnati Liberty Hall* on the strange illness. The article opined that those who abstained from meat and milk products in late summer and fall did not suffer the disease. However, the *Medical Repository*'s total circulation by its second year of publication was approximately three hundred subscribers. Most likely, very few of those subscribers lived west of the Alleghenies or took note of the article.

Any further mention of the mystifying illness failed to make its way into New England newspapers or medical journals, because cases were not being reported in those areas. And since Europeans had never encountered the disease, the European medical community ignored any investigation of the illness.

Bourbon County physician Thomas Barbee first reported the "trembles" after visiting settlements around the Miami River in southwestern Ohio. Only one physician in the medical community seemed to be interested in Barbee's report: Dr. Daniel Drake. In 1810 Drake reproduced Barbee's entire report about the bizarre affliction in an essay titled "Notices Concerning Cincinnati" "so that physicians may determine how far it deserves the appellation of a new disease."

Drake, a native of New Jersey, settled in Mayslick, Kentucky, with his family at a young age, eventually leaving the

Eng.d by A.H Rutchie

Daniel Drake

GREVE, CHARLES THEODORE (1904) CENTENNIAL HISTORY OF CINCINNATI AND REPRESENTATIVE CITIZENS I

community at age sixteen to study medicine in Cincinnati. Four years later Drake left Cincinnati to attend the University of Pennsylvania medical school. After taking two medical courses, he came back to Mayslick to practice medicine before relocating to

Cincinnati. Drake became an influential medical authority who successfully founded and obtained state funding for the Ohio State Medical Society and the Medical College of Ohio, now known as the University of Cincinnati Academic Health Center.

Drake began documenting outbreaks of the mystifying disease while he was traveling through the area in 1822. He also began reporting observations in medical journals, most notably his own publication, *Western Journal of the Medicine and Physical Sciences.* He believed animals contracted the disease by eating some type of plant and transmitted the illness through human consumption of meat, milk, or butter.

For the treatment of humans afflicted with the disease, Drake advised attending physicians to keep the patient's bowels open and have them avoid heavy meals and curtail any strenuous exercise. Sodium chloride, sodium bicarbonate administered orally or by enema, and molasses enemas were viewed as successful treatments.

The disease's connection with milk heightened as cases linked milk consumption with the illness, and symptoms gained attention. The illness named the "trembles" was eventually dubbed "milk sickness," but Barbee and Drake had not definitively associated it with milk. Other terms associated with the disease included "sick stomach," "puking illness," and the "slows." It was noted that children who vomited immediately after drinking affected milk recovered from the disease much better than adults, because the youngsters had much "stronger stomachs." Another observation noted that cows giving milk were the last in a herd to die of the disease. The doctors reasoned this was the case because the poison was excreted in the milk. Others noted that cattle confined at night seldom acquired the disease, and cows left in cultivated fields never got the illness.

Milk sickness outbreaks soon became endemic in the early nineteenth century, starting north of the Ohio River and quickly moving farther south. In 1818 Nancy Hanks Lincoln, the mother of Abraham Lincoln, died from the rampage of milk sickness that afflicted her pioneer community in Spencer County, Indiana. Hysteria about the disease prompted many with confirmed cases to leave villages or towns.

Until 1835, the causes of milk sickness centered around three possibilities: a germ, poisonous minerals, or a poisonous plant. The germ or "bad air" theory was a common belief among settlers who postulated the causes of illness, death, and general bad luck when scientific evidence was lacking. Early theorists, including the editor of the *Philadelphia Journal of the Medical and Physical Sciences,* postulated that a "miasmatic or noxious exhalation" rose from wooded mountain ravines strong enough to kill an entire herd of cattle.

Others opined that a bacterium, specifically *bacillus lactomorbus,* was the culprit. Bacteria supporters believed there was a connection between milk sickness and malaria. However, scientists determined it was improbable that *bacillus lactomorbus* could randomly strike such a wide spectrum of a geographic region. Others studied samples of water from the Scioto River and afflicted patients' urine, noting both samples exhibited the same spiral and sphero bacteria. These scientists concluded a germ derived from drinking water and vegetables washed or watered with contaminated water spread the disease. Others believed some sort of divine providence or, worse, magical witches, tainted the soil with the germ.

Still others contended a poisonous mineral was the basis for the disease. These proponents hypothesized that since cattle grazing unattended at night were more prone to the disease, some mysterious poison must have been tainting the nightly dew. A North Carolina etiologist even believed arsenic was the culprit. He noted copper deposits were evident in areas where milk-sickness outbreaks took place. He theorized that the heat of the sun had the capacity to break arsenic from the copper and tinge the dew with the poison. However, this theory proved pointless when outbreaks occurred in all regions of Kentucky, whether or not copper was evident in the geological layers of the regional topography. For example, cases sprouted in glacial regions of Boone and Campbell Counties (Orthovician); Monroe and Todd Counties (Carboniferous); Henderson and Davis Counties (Silurian); and Graves County (Quaternary). Drake even discredited this theory, noting many grazing areas were situated on secondary limestone and were not poisoned by the rock. Sulfate zinc found in suspected areas also caused symptoms similar to the "trembles," but such places were not conducive for grazing. Still others blamed a poisonous fungus.

A poisonous plant was the most widely accepted suspect. However, narrowing the wide range of plants to one specific culprit was the problem. Plants considered top suspects included poison oak, wild parsnip, *Rhus radicans* vine, and white snakeroot. At one point Drake identified poison oak as the cause, but his testing of this hypothesis failed to produce any conclusive evidence.

In 1828, Illinois physician Anna Pierce Hobbs Bigby noted a Shawnee Indian had told her that white snakeroot was the culprit. Although she wrote of her discovery to her medical colleagues back East, her work went unnoticed. A decade later Ohio farmer John Rowe also suspected white snakeroot as the cause. He told a local newspaper that he had fed white snakeroot to two cows and a calf, killing all three. A local physician performed a postmortem on one of Rowe's animals as a measure of additional evidence. But Drake dismissed the theory, noting other farmers let their animals graze in pastures of wild white snakeroot without any sign of the "trembles." Claiming Rowe's lack of written experiment and subsequent controlled observation, Drake sarcastically noted, "A professional scrutiny only can be relied on in such cases. The testimony adduced by Mr. Rowe is, therefore, defective."

The key problem in identifying a plant poison was the fact that a suspected plant often had numerous variations. John Rowe's belief that white snakeroot was the cause of milk sickness was difficult to prove. White snakeroot was originally classified as part of the genus *Eupatorium rugosum,* which was later changed to *Ageratina altissima.* White snakeroot comes from the aster family and is also known as richweed, fall poison, white topped deerwort/boneset, squawweed, and other names. Characterized by white flowers and a fragrant odor, the plant was known to have as many as forty species in the South. Moreover, thirty species contained white flowers synonymous with white snakeroot.

In 1830, Henderson County residents along the Green River were particularly hard hit by milk sickness. This epidemic may have prompted the state legislature of Kentucky to offer a six hundred dollar reward to anyone who could discover the cause of the disease and prove a successful cure. When no one came forth with a plausible solution, the state legislature boosted the reward to two thousand dollars in February 1841 for anyone who could pinpoint the cause within five years. Reward claimants were required to have their documentation verified by a panel of thirty-four physicians selected by the legislature from twenty counties. If two or more individuals successfully offered the same conclusions, the reward would be granted to the first claimant. Whether enticed by the reward or the greater medical good, Drake set out on a fifteen-day trip in September 1841, traveling by horseback and foot for more than 150 miles from Cincinnati, northeast along the Scioto River, then west by the Little Miami River, in search of any etiological or pathophysiological evidence for the disease.

The first time the disease was written into a medical textbook was in 1848, courtesy of Drake's quest seven years earlier. Even when milk sickness was mentioned in medical texts, medical writers who had been contracted by publishing houses in the East had never actually treated patients with the disease, because it primarily afflicted residents of the West. One medical writer, George Wood, noted he had never seen a case of milk sickness, but included seven pages of discussion of the disease and cited key authors on the subject.

By the time the disease appeared in medical publications, however, it had begun to subside. In fact between 1850 and 1900, milk-sickness outbreaks increasingly declined. Isolated cases made their way into medical journals, but it wasn't until 1926 that science formally determined white snakeroot as the milk sickness culprit. A US Department of Agriculture scientist, Dr. James Couch, successfully isolated the toxic alcohol tremetol from white snakeroot. Couch determined that the poisonous alcohol evaporated as the plants completely dried, making the plant unable to transmit milk sickness. Since white snakeroot loses its tremetol upon drying, spring rain showers and summer thunderstorms fed the growth of the plant and its toxin. When cases of milk sickness occurred in the winter, its occurrence may have been attributed to the fact that white snakeroot could grow up to five feet high, easily catching the eyes of a hungry herd.

White snakeroot grows as far south as Texas and as far north as North Dakota, with a greater concentration in Kentucky, Ohio,

Indiana, and Illinois. Resilient in most growing conditions, white snakeroot is prevalent in open shade areas, woodland borders, bluffs, and ravines. One of Kentucky's fastest-growing plants, white snakeroot is pollinated by a host of insects such as bees, wasps, butterflies, and moths; it spreads easily, through either airborne seeds or a vast root network. The roots are the most toxic part of the plant. However, many settlers and Native Americans often ground the plant's roots to use as a medicinal covering to cure snakebites. Native Americans also used the plant's leaves for a tea to treat diarrhea and kidney stones. Moreover, burning white snakeroot leaves would often revive comatose patients.

The plant thrives in damp forest conditions, and settlers often left their cattle and other farm animals unattended in open uncultivated fields—conditions ripe for milk sickness to flourish. Humans acquired the disease by eating tainted meat, milk, butter, or cheese. Since white snakeroot has shallow roots, fencing off or eradicating the plant from farmland was not difficult. As farms became cultivated with defined acreage marked by fences and cleared of forested areas, milk sickness began to wane. Besides agricultural practices, milk pasteurization further thwarted the spread of the toxin. Couch learned from his research that pasteurization temperatures were not high enough to decompose tremetol, but the temperature to cook meat was sufficient for getting rid of the toxin.

Today researchers know that many of the symptoms of milk sickness mirror those of patients suffering from starvation and diabetes mellitus. Tremetol poisoning suppresses an intracellular critical enzyme responsible for converting acid food into energy. Tremetol produces ketoacidosis, a condition that raises the level of fat while decreasing the rate of carbohydrate metabolism. When carbohydrate metabolism fails, an excessive amount of fatty lipids are stored in the liver. An increase in acetone occurs, and an accumulation of ketone builds in the blood, precipitating the need to urinate. Acetone is also eliminated through breathing, causing the afflicted to transmit a sweet, garlicky smell.

A buildup of lactic acid produces stiffening in the muscles. Milk sickness death is attributed to fatty buildup in the liver and kidneys. When scientists examined human patients postmortem, they noted fatty degeneration of all tissues, as well as the pronounced odor of acetone in the stomach. One researcher found fatty buildup in the brain of a human victim, but was unable to examine this evidence in other victims because of outcries from local citizens.

The last reported case of milk sickness occurred in two infants in St. Louis in 1963. Currently tremetol may be found when a single cow or small herd is used for a raw milk supply, but the practice of pooling milk from a large herd dilutes any toxins. Tremetol poisoning is now treated by administering appropriate doses of sodium lactate, glucose, and hypotonic Ringer's solution.

CHAPTER 6

Mike Fink: The Legendary "Mississippi River Alligator Horse"

Respect for the law was not one of Mike Fink's admirable traits. A hard-drinking, gambling, roustabout boatman, Fink became well-known during the early nineteenth century for his practical jokes, bravado, and ability to handle a fight with anyone. He symbolized the uncouth frontiersmen who lived a transient lifestyle fighting Indians and untamed rivers. And his antics became legendary, mixed with both fact and fiction, as he brandished his own sense of law and order.

One of the best examples of Fink's disrespect for the law occurred when a Louisville constable summoned him to court for a long-awaited trial. Falling on hard times, the constable thought the best way to feed his family was to reap a reward for Fink's capture. During a moment of sentimentality, Fink agreed to come to court under one condition. Since his keelboat and boatmen were his only family, he insisted on arriving with his yawl in tow! Eager to detain the wayward boatman, the constable consented.

A long-coupled wagon and herd of oxen went down Third Street to fetch Fink's keelboat. Considering the road was unpaved by modern standards, the wharf was steep and muddy. Despite the conditions, the boat was positioned onto the wagon with Fink and his men atop it with long poles descending into the mud, like slalom snow skiers. Fink shouted out to his men, "Set poles!" and every pole was dug into the mud. "Back her!" he roared. Back down the hill slid the wagon, yawl, men, and oxen. By the third attempt, Fink began to doubt his joke would actually work and suspected one of his men could be injured in the process. However, the efforts of this seesawing movement actually jockeyed the wagon up the hill by the third try.

Fink, his crew, and keelboat made their way along Third Street to the courthouse, certainly with plenty of sightseers along the way. Inside the Louisville courtroom, Fink was acquitted for lack of sufficient evidence on one indictment, but was found guilty for others. Figuring he had more important things to do, Fink decided not to wait to hear the judgments on those cases. He gave a signal to his men to board and be prepared to lift anchor to his landed vessel. Considering the first adventure down Third Street, Fink's crew did not relish the return to the wharf. Facing Fink's temper if they refused, however, would be a far worse alternative. Fink waved his red bandanna affixed to a red pole and summoned his men to use their poles to move his vessel back to shore. As he left, Fink promised he would call again.

Who was Mike Fink? Was he real or a legend?

He was actually a little of both. Born near Fort Pitt, between 1770 and 1780, Fink grew up on the western edge of Pennsylvania. Fort Pitt had been the center of the British conference with the Delawares, Shawnees, Mingoes, and Mohicans but experienced some quiet before the Lord Dunmore Wars began in 1774. The supply and rendezvous encampment attracted many settlers, vagabonds, traders, and boatmen. The confluence of the Allegheny, Monongahela, and Ohio Rivers solidified the area surrounding Fort Pitt as a keelboat and flatboat hub. With the Indian activity circumventing around Fort Pitt, Fink naturally fit into the role of an Indian scout. He excelled in marksmanship, and some accounts claim he was even forbidden to enter shooting competitions at Fort Pitt for fear he would drive off other competitors.

Fink shunned the farming lifestyle that was transforming the area around Fort Pitt into the early vestiges of Pittsburgh. He started boating up and down the Ohio River and eventually gained business acumen in the trade. Around 1810 he purchased two keelboats and headquartered his business in West Virginia. When the river became too low for navigation, Fink spent his time honing his rifle skills. He easily worked for whiskey and crowd enjoyment. He stood approximately six feet, three inches tall and weighed 180 pounds, well proportioned for the physical rigors of managing keelboat poles and fending off a drunken attacker. His pleasant features—blue expressive eyes, olive skin, and broad white teeth—combined with his strength and ability made some liken him to Hercules or another ancient god.

Dubbed half-horse, half-alligator, Fink's counterpart boatmen were illiterate men who eked out a living by working among the fringes of society. They played in the same manner as they lived. The "alligator horse" moniker arose from Andrew Jackson's militiamen exploits at the Battle of New Orleans in 1815, when their four-thousand-man force won a decisive victory over a British contingent approximately twice the American's size. The term emphasized the strength and amphibious nature of living and fighting in the swamps of Louisiana. In his *Hunters of Kentucky,* Samuel Woodworth composed a ballad describing the Kentucky troops who fought in the battle as "ev'ry man was half a horse, and half an alligator." The first time the song was performed in New Orleans around 1820, the audience, crowded with river men, rose from their seats in approval of the ballad. Noah Ludlow, the performer, remarked, "The whole pit was standing up and shouting. I had to sing it three times that night before they would let me off." Andrew Jackson himself used the song when he ran his 1828 presidential campaign.

Mike Fink's anecdotes circulated through oral tradition. The first published story featuring Fink was Morgan Neville's *The Last of the Boatmen* in 1828, which was a sketch depicting life on the Ohio River. The first performance featuring Mike Fink was Alphonso Wetmore's 1821 low-comedy production titled *The Pedlar,* whose character is portrayed as a bully and braggart.

Various authors transposed oral tales about Fink's legendary escapades into written form, embellishing facts and blurring the lines between truth and fiction. Fink left no known proof he ever married or had a family, but stories handed down indicated he always had a woman by his side and, possibly, children by several women. These close relationships were often the butt of some of his jokes. For example, one of his girlfriends was resigned to holding a tin cup full of whiskey atop her head while Fink practiced shooting the cup off her head. Another one of his exploits included her holding the cup between her knees or in a vise. Mirroring his alligator horse persona, Fink reportedly had a huge daughter who could whistle out of one corner of her mouth, eat with the other, and scream with the middle. She could even tame a wild bear.

Many of Fink's pranks are certainly considered sexist by today's standards. According to one anecdote, he landed his boat at the mouth of the Muskingum and Ohio Rivers in late autumn with little or no food left on board. He disembarked the boat and collected dried beech leaves into an oblong ring taller than his head. None of his crew understood his actions, nor did he explain his purpose. Fink tested the strength of the pile by jumping on top of it. Getting up, he went aboard his keelboat, grabbed his rifle, and summoned his wife to follow him. In a characteristically machismo voice, Fink ordered her to get into the pile and lie down. She replied, "Now, Mr. Fink, what have I done? I don't know, I'm sure!" Fink cut her off and demanded she get in or he would shoot her.

His wife obeyed and crawled into the leaf pile. Fink covered the pile with splinters of a flour barrel and deliberately set four corners of the leaf pile on fire. Winds instantly sprung up and spread the fire across the entire leaf pile. Fink stood silently, watching to see how long it would take for his wife to escape. When the flames became too intense, she bolted from the pile and plunged into the river with hair and clothing aflame. "There," said Fink, "that'll larn you not to be winkin' at them fellers on t'other boat." Such displays of dictatorial brutishness epitomized the boatman's lifestyle of lawlessness, rudeness, and power.

Endemic of the racism of the time, Fink's pranks also targeted Indians. According to one account, Fink shot an Indian at the same moment the Indian fired at a deer. Having left his boat to hunt game, Fink spotted a deer—and an Indian intent on the same deer. Fink shrank behind a tree and watched the Indian move positions to gain a better target. The Indian halted a few paces, leveled his gun, and shot at the deer. At the same moment, Fink raised his gun and shot the Indian in the chest. Upon returning to his boat, Fink boasted he had taken down both the Indian and the deer with one bullet. Fink bragged, "Hurray for me, you scapegoats! I'm a land-screamer. I'm a water dog. I'm a snapping turtle. I can lick five times my own weight in wildcats, I can use up Injens by the cord. I can swallow niggers whole, raw, or cooked. I can out-run, out-dance, out-jump, out-dive, out-drink, out-holler, and out-lick any white thing in the shape o' human that's ever put a foot within two thousand miles o' the big Massassip."

Another yarn about Fink's insulting treatment of Indians appeared in the July 16, 1842, edition of the *Spirit of the Times,* a magazine that published many of the best anecdotes and tales of the era. As the story goes, Fink moored near Louisville and developed an affinity for humiliating an aging but destitute Cherokee named Proud Joe. The Indian wore a signature scalp lock with an accompanying hawk feather. One day Fink mockingly plucked the hawk feather from the adornment, quickly drawing the ire of the old Cherokee. A few days later, prior to leaving shore, Fink aimed his firearm at Proud Joe's adorned scalp lock from the shoreline with the intent of taking it out. Once the gun fired, Proud Joe dropped to the ground among a crowd of onlookers. Surprised by his feat, Fink fled with rifle in hand into the Ohio River. The crowds, amazed by the callous brazenness of the action, quickly chased Fink into the water. Fink made his way to a skiff and turned his rifle onto his pursuers, who immediately called off the hunt. Back on shore the crowd gasped with amazement at the sight of the assumed dead Cherokee rising to his feet—and the realization that his scalp lock had been shot right from his head.

Fink's recklessness also weighed against blacks, casting racial overtones in its barbaric humor. According to a tall tale published in several newspapers and magazines during the 1840s, a black man ventured down the Mississippi River shoreline

Mike Fink's Great Shot (1854)

Thomas Bangs Thorpe (1815–1878)

where Fink's boat was moored, hoping to catch a closer view of the vessel. Fink watched the man, eventually raising his rifle to his shoulder and firing on the man's heel. The black man cried murder when he realized his heel had been severed. Fink claimed he just shot at the man "so he kin wear a decent boot." Eventually apprehended and brought before a judge in St. Louis, Fink demanded the judge compensate him "fur trimmin' the heel of one of your own town niggers." Fink eventually paid the black man several pieces of silver in restitution for the ruthless prank.

Some of Fink's pranks were not nearly as barbaric, but revered for acts of skill. Such feats were particularly respected traits by Americans who were spreading into untamed parts of the country. Tales of his antics were told and retold, often exaggerated in written formats with authors adding their own embellishments. Fink appeared often as Davy Crockett's nemesis in the *Crockett Almanac,* a popular magazine mass-produced between 1835 and 1856 that chronicled fictional accounts of Crockett's western adventures. Claims of Fink's skills included feats such as consuming a gallon of whiskey in twenty-four hours, taking a flatboat over the Falls of the Ohio, riding a moose like a horse, and drowning an attacking female wolf while canoeing in the Mississippi River. He reportedly even battled river pirates holed up at Cave-in-Rock on the Ohio River.

In another reported incident, Fink was leisurely swimming when a ferocious bull attacked him. Fink managed to mount the animal's back to rein the bull, only to run into a hornet's nest in the melee. Fink found himself hanging onto the bull's tail, clinging for dear life. He later reportedly recalled: "He drug me over every brier and stump in the field until I was sweatin' and bleedin' like a fat bear with a pack o' hounds at his heels. And my name ain't Mike Fink, if the old critter's tail and I didn't blow out sometimes at a dead level with the varmint's back."

Much in the same manner as church revivals added excitement to an otherwise solitary and dangerous settler's way of life, Mike Fink's escapades brought comic relief to frontiersmen who ventured into unknown and tenuous locales. Ingenuity and the ability to think and act quickly were a matter of both life and death to backwoodsmen. Even newspaper humorists picked up on Fink's "alligator horse" persona and published his escapades in a serial titled "King of the Keelboatmen" during the 1850s.

A fine example of Fink's mischievous side is the tale of the boatman eyeing a large flock of sheep grazing along the river shore. Desiring fresh meat, Fink moored at a nearby eddy, found some scotch snuff in his cargo, and went ashore. He caught five to six sheep and rubbed their faces thoroughly with the snuff. Returning to the boat, he told his crew to quickly go to the farmer's home and tell him to check his sheep. The farmer immediately noticed some of his flock were rubbing their noses to the ground and behaving as though they were out of their minds.

When the farmer questioned if anyone knew or saw what happened, Fink explained the sheep must have been afflicted with a disease known as black murrain. Asked if he knew how to cure the disease, Fink replied, "Only one as I knows of . . . better shoot 'em right-off; they've got to die any way." The farmer was unsure whether the afflicted sheep could be singled out from among the flock, but Fink reassured him that it was possible. And with payment of a couple of gallons of old peach brandy, Fink shot the sheep and disposed of them into the eddy. After dark Fink and his crew hauled the sheep onto the boat, packed the meat, and went merrily on their way the next day.

Sometimes Fink was the receiver of his own pranks. In one recorded account that appeared in several publications during the mid-nineteenth century, Fink was head butted by fellow flatboatman Jack Pierce. Pierce, a champion ram butter, dealt three successive blows to Fink. Onlookers described the noise as sounding like an axe striking timber. Although Fink survived, Pierce relished in the victory.

Fink continued his debauchery the farther west he ventured, but his demise began as steamboats quickly overtook the keelboat industry. In one telling episode, Fink refused to move his keelboat to the side of the channel as he eyed a steamboat advancing upstream. As the approaching steamboat blared its horn, plenty of men on deck screamed for the keelboat to get out of the way. Fink paid no attention and stood resolutely at his keelboat's stern, awaiting the steamboat's crushing blow. The collision hurled the steamboat chimney overboard, tore the larboard guard to pieces, and forced a gaping hole in the bow. "Keel's sinking, Mike!" yelled his crewmen. Fink smiled savagely and directed the bow toward the bank. However, a large portion of his freight was lead, and unavoidable disaster occurred within seconds.

After the steamboat dethroned the keelboat for river trading, Fink moved onto a third trade, fur trapping, and ventured west into Missouri in 1822. But his raucous life of drinking and fighting as a river roustabout began to take its toll. Together with two friends, Carpenter and Talbot, Fink joined William Ashley and Major Andrew Henry's company of Missouri trappers and traveled up the Missouri River to Fort William Henry at the mouth of the Yellowstone River. The fort was a center hub for trappers, but Fink, Carpenter, and Talbot preferred keeping to themselves and living off the fort grounds along a nearby river bluff. One of the men's favorite pastimes was placing a tin cup of whiskey on each other's heads and taking turns shooting it at a distance of up to seventy yards. As skilled trappers the men never seemed to miss their mark. But a death premonition prompted Carpenter to bequeath his pistol, gun, and wages to Talbot in case he should die.

During one particular drunken moment of camaraderie, the men placed a tin cup of whiskey on Carpenter's head. After fixing his aim, Fink took down his gun and laughingly cried, "Hold your noddle steady, Carpenter, and don't spill the whisky, for I shall want some presently." Pulling the trigger, Fink missed his mark and fatally shot Carpenter in the forehead. Unable to believe he had erred in his target, he said, "I took as fair a bead on the black spot on the cup as I ever took on a squirrel's eye."

Several months after Carpenter's death, Talbot overheard a drunken Fink boast that he had killed Carpenter intentionally. Enraged, Talbot drew the pistol that Carpenter had bequeathed to him and shot Fink in the heart.

Death cemented the folklore of Mike Fink into publication—but historians have never been able to discern fact from fiction regarding almost every aspect of his life and death. Historical researchers, for example, contend that they have discovered at least five various accounts of his demise. Even the date of Fink's death remains uncertain, with estimates ranging from 1823 to 1848.

The popularity of tall tales about Mike Fink had faded by the onset of the Civil War. Americans grew tired of Fink's backwoodsmen antics as the winds of an impending war swept through the nation. But the legend of Mike Fink continued to live on in the oral stories about the king of the boatmen.

CHAPTER 7

The Ghosts of Liberty Hall

One of the oldest brick homes in Frankfort, Liberty Hall was built by Kentucky's first US Senator, John Brown. During the first half of the nineteenth century, the exquisite Federal-style home welcomed guests ranging from America's early statesmen to extended members of the Brown family. And according to legends and eyewitnesses, the spirits of several guests may have never left the premises.

In 1796 John Brown purchased four acres of land in Frankfort and started the construction of his personal residence on the property. Brown named the home in honor of Liberty Hall Academy, a Virginia school founded by his father, an Irish immigrant and Presbyterian minister who had served as the schoolmaster. A Virginia native, Brown attended the College of New Jersey, now known as Princeton, and studied law at William and Mary until his studies were interrupted by the arrival of British forces in the fall of 1780. He completed his studies in the law offices of Thomas Jefferson near Charlottesville, Virginia.

John Brown opened his own law office in Danville, Kentucky, during the early 1780s and joined the local Political Club, an organization devoted to transforming Kentucky into a state. In 1787 Brown represented the county of Kentucky, which was situated within the state of Virginia, at the Continental Congress. The following year, he was elected to serve as a US congressman under the new Constitution. During his term of office, he successfully petitioned Congress to separate the county of Kentucky from the state of Virginia. In June 1792 Kentucky became the fifteenth state, and Brown became Kentucky's first US senator.

In 1798 Brown met Margaretta Mason, a twenty-five-year-old New Yorker, through mutual friends in New York. Like Brown, the young woman was also the child of a Presbyterian minister. Her father, John Mason, had been George Washington's chaplain at West Point. Though Brown was fifteen years older than Margaretta, romance blossomed quickly, and the couple married in February 1799. Since Brown's magnificent Frankfort home was still under construction, the couple began their married life near the nation's capital in Philadelphia and welcomed their first son, Mason, into the world in November 1799. With the completion of the US Capitol in 1800, the Browns moved from their temporary home in Philadelphia to the new capital city of Washington, DC.

In the spring of 1801, the family settled into their new home in Frankfort. Only the finest materials had been used in

Liberty Hall in Frankfort, Kentucky

the construction of the mansion, which took nearly five years to complete. Bricks for the exterior, made of clay dug from the cellar, were fired on-site, while hardwood for the flooring, rafters, and framing had been dried for over two years before being used in construction. With Brown's close ties to Thomas Jefferson, some historians speculate that Jefferson may have designed Liberty Hall. Although the true identity of the architect has never been substantiated, other researchers believe that Brown himself may have drawn the plans.

A few months after moving into Liberty Hall, the Browns became the proud parents of a second son, Orlando, on September 26, 1801. Shortly after his son's birth, Brown left Frankfort and returned to work in Washington. With her husband back in the Senate, Margaretta focused on furnishing and decorating Liberty Hall.

Bringing a touch of New York style to the frontier nature of Frankfort, Margaretta spared no expense in furnishing her new home. She decorated the elegant mansion with fine silk fabrics and Parisian furnishings brought back to the United States by the senator's brother, James Brown, who served as the ambassador to France during President James Monroe's administration.

The Browns also added outbuildings on the property, including a kitchen and laundry, a smokehouse, a privy, stables, a carriage house, and slave quarters. Since the property bordered the Kentucky River, they built stairs from the garden to the river and constructed a boat landing.

While her husband continued his political career in Washington, Margaretta continued to run the household in Frankfort. She also gave birth to two more sons, one in 1803 and another in 1804. Unfortunately, the infants—both named Alfred—lived only a few months. Grieving from the devastating losses, Margaretta lapsed into a deep depression. To make matters worse, Brown lost his bid for another term in the Senate in 1805. During his tenure as a senator, he was named president pro tempore twice.

Back in Frankfort, Brown remained active in the community. He became a founding member of the Frankfort Water Company and director of the first Bank of Kentucky. He also managed hundreds of acres of property in central Kentucky and twenty thousand acres near Chillicothe, Ohio. He even purchased a ferry for crossing the Kentucky River, and he supervised the construction of a public church and Kentucky's Capitol building in Frankfort.

The Browns rejoiced at the birth of their only daughter, Euphemia Helen, on May 14, 1807. But tragedy struck the family again when a high fever resulted in the young girl's death on October 1, 1814. According to one historical account, the Brown's daughter died from an overdose of mercury chloride, a popular treatment of the time.

In spite of the sadness of losing three children, John and Margaretta eventually resumed an active social life and entertained many of the nation's leaders at Liberty Hall. In 1819, for example, President James Monroe and two future chief executives—Colonel Zachary Taylor and Colonel Andrew Jackson—visited the Browns' Frankfort mansion. In 1825 the Marquis de Lafayette attended a ball given in his honor at Liberty Hall. Other guests at Liberty Hall throughout the years included Aaron Burr, William Henry Harrison, and Theodore Roosevelt.

Margaret Verrick, Margaretta's aunt, traveled from New York in 1817 to visit her niece in Frankfort. Some historical accounts contend that Verrick had raised Margaretta after the death of her mother, so the two women may have had a particularly close relationship. Other versions of the story claim that Verrick made the trip to comfort her niece as she mourned the death of her young daughter. Unfortunately the journey of eight hundred miles, most likely by stagecoach and horseback, took its toll on the sixty-five-year-old aunt. Only three days after her arrival in Frankfort, Verrick suffered a heart attack and died in an upstairs bedroom at Liberty Hall. She was buried in a small family cemetery near the home's gardens. Apparently her grave was not marked, because questions later arose about the exact location of her remains on the property.

In 1826 John and Margaretta became grandparents with the birth of Benjamin Gratz Brown, the child of their eldest son Mason and his wife Judith Bledsoe. When Judith died a year later, Margaretta raised Benjamin until Mason remarried in 1835.

John Brown died in 1837 at age eighty, and his wife passed away the following year. Their son Mason inherited Liberty Hall and lived there until his death in 1867. Following Mason's death, descendants of Senator and Margaretta Brown continued to occupy the home.

After Verrick's death, members of the community heard reports that Margaretta's Aunt Margaret was still making her presence known at Liberty Hall. Local lore contended that her soul remained in the house, caring for anyone who might need help. Several descendants of John and Margaretta were the first to allege a ghostly presence at the Frankfort mansion. As the bride of Benjamin Gratz Brown slept in the room where Aunt Margaret had died, she awoke to see the figure of a woman in a gray dress walking quietly across the room. Another version of this story reported the young woman awoke to the feeling of someone touching her hand. When she opened her eyes, she saw a woman with gray hair, clad in a gray dress that softly rustled as she walked. The misty gray figure soon became known as the "Gray Lady."

Benjamin Gratz Brown's sister, also named Margaretta Brown, claimed to have seen the Gray Lady, as did a friend, Rebecca Averill of Frankfort. As an overnight guest at Liberty Hall, Averill claimed that she saw the Gray Lady standing quietly next to the fireplace in her bedroom. Quickly pulling the sheets over her head, the young woman prayed the ghostly figure would disappear. When she gathered up the courage to look across the room again, she realized her prayer had been answered and breathed a sigh of relief.

Mary Mason Scott, a great-granddaughter of Senator Brown, also saw her ancestor on several occasions. According to one account, Miss Scott had not been aware of a ghostly presence at Liberty Hall until she returned home from college. On the first night of her return to the Frankfort home, she slept in Aunt Margaret's bedchambers. Within a few hours she awoke to find the grayish vision of a matronly ghost standing next to the bed. One local story of the time contended that the Gray Lady was using Scott as a "medium" to find the location of her unmarked grave. Moreover, it was reported that Scott bore a remarkable resemblance to her ancestor.

Members of the Brown family claimed to have seen the Gray Lady in every room of Liberty Hall, although her presence has been felt or seen most often in the upstairs bedroom where she took her final breath. Her ghost has been described as a neatly dressed small figure with a nonthreatening, calming demeanor. She has even been seen performing household chores. Overnight guests sometimes awoke to find themselves being tucked in by a smiling woman; in the morning they may have found blankets folded or some mending completed. Other visitors claimed that doors would close and rocking chairs would move without any signs of wind.

In 1922 Mary Mason Scott and her brother John Matthew Scott, John and Margaretta Brown's great-grandchildren, announced plans to donate their family home to a nonprofit organization upon their deaths, with the stipulation that Liberty Hall be maintained as a museum home. One newspaper termed the mansion a "genuine treasure," while another asserted that it contained "more genuine antiques and actual heirlooms than probably any other home in Kentucky."

When Mary Mason Scott, the last resident of Liberty Hall, died in 1934, she left the family mansion to her brother. In 1937, John Matthew Scott deeded the property to Liberty Hall, Inc., a nonprofit organization formed for the purpose of opening the house as a museum. In 1956 Liberty Hall, Inc. turned over control of the property to the National Society of the Colonial Dames of America in the Commonwealth of Kentucky. Today the Colonial Dames operate Liberty Hall as a living museum of Kentucky history.

Unexplainable happenings continued to occur at the magnificent mansion throughout the twentieth century. The family living directly across from the mansion asserted they would often be sitting on the front porch in the evening and see candlelight flickering through the rooms on both floors of Liberty Hall.

People passing by Liberty Hall reported that they saw Aunt Margaret peering out of an upstairs window. One college professor suspected moonlight may be the cause of the Gray Lady's appearances in the window and was permitted to stay in the house for six weeks, during an entire moon phase. He found the moonlight did not cause any unusual reflections in the windowpane. But on one of his last nights in Liberty Hall, the man was startled awake by a touch. Standing beside him was the Gray Lady, smiling faintly.

In 1964 a team of parapsychologists and a member of the National Historical Society stayed at Liberty Hall for one week to record any strange events occurring after dark. The parapsychologists claimed they often saw a grayish mist floating through the halls and rooms, especially around the niece's room.

Some of the strongest evidence for a haunting at Liberty Hall occurred in 1965. Though quickly reported and extinguished, a fire at Liberty Hall destroyed a hallway and several pieces of antique furniture. Two men, a Frankfort fireman and a local newspaper employee, volunteered to stay in the house at night to guard against vandalism.

With no electricity to light their way through the building, the men placed candles in the rooms and on the stairs. Exploring the house on the first night of their stay, they climbed into the attic. As they looked around the area, the attic door slammed shut behind them. The men tugged at the door until it opened, hastily closed the door behind them, and ran down the stairs. When they returned later that evening, they discovered the attic door had been opened again, though they were certain they had closed the door behind them.

The next evening the men found the same door open. Once again they closed the door, only to return and find it open a few hours later. On their third and final evening at Liberty Hall, the same mysterious events occurred, along with the sounds of eerie cries, moans, and groans. Moreover, candles were suddenly extinguished with no explanation.

The following year another unexplainable event occurred at Liberty Hall. The curator discovered three gold bracelets on a nightstand in the upstairs "ghost" bedroom. Liberty Hall had not been open for tours during the cold, snowy month of January, so a forgetful tourist could not have left the jewelry in the room. The curator could not find the jewelry listed in the house inventory, and none of the staff recognized the bracelets or knew why they had appeared on the table. She took them to a jeweler, who determined they were made in New York before 1800, a few years before Aunt Margaret visited her niece.

During restoration of Liberty Hall in the 1970s, the same curator took pictures of the work inside the home. One photograph taken after the restoration of the main staircase revealed the faint image of a woman walking down the stairs. When the curator had snapped the picture, no one had been standing in front of the camera.

During the early 1980s, a Colonial Dames employee recounted her experiences of living in a small apartment above Liberty Hall's kitchen. This same employee often portrayed the Gray Lady at Halloween, dressed in period attire, walking back and forth in front of a window with a lighted candle in her hand. Though she admitted that she never actually saw the real Gray Lady, she was certain of the ghost's presence in the mansion. Taking a bath late one evening, she left the bathroom door open. As she washed her hair, the door closed by itself. The large, heavy door had never opened or closed on its own before that evening.

The employee encountered other strange experiences while living in the house, as well, including a library door that some-times opened and closed without warning. Once, she wistfully thought about an old boyfriend who had presented her with a box that played beautiful music upon opening the lid. Though she had owned the gift for years, she had not opened or wound the music box for some time. But as she thought about the old boyfriend's gift, the music box began to play, even though the lid was still tightly shut.

Since then ghostly phenomena have been frequently reported at Liberty Hall. Oftentimes staff members have felt an eerie presence when doors open and close mysteriously or when lights flicker in empty rooms. Some people have experienced chills standing in certain parts of the house. In the summer of 2000, a Windsor chair on the second floor was moved into the middle of the room. None of the staff admitted to the prank.

Though Aunt Margaret is the most famous ghost at Liberty Hall, other spirits may also inhabit the grand estate. In 1805 a Spanish opera singer from New Orleans visited the Browns at their home. According to one account, the Browns invited the woman to perform at their home. Another version of the legend reveals John and Margaretta hosted a party at Liberty Hall in honor of the young soprano who was performing elsewhere in Frankfort. At some point during the gala event, the singer stepped out into the gardens for a breath of fresh air. Since the evening was hot and humid, guests at the party did not question the woman's actions—until she vanished from sight. Eyewitnesses claimed their last glimpse of the dark-haired beauty was her lone figure strolling toward the river at the edge of Liberty Hall's gardens. Could she have slipped from the riverbank and fallen into the water? No trace of her was ever found, despite extensive searches of the Kentucky River. Since Frankfort was nothing more than a frontier settlement in 1805, could she have been attacked and abducted by a band of ruffians? Some people theorized a roving tribe of Indians, attracted to Liberty Hall by the lights and party sounds, may have seized the opportunity to snatch up an attractive young woman who was walking alone.

In later years someone spotted a dark-haired apparition running through the Liberty Hall gardens on hot, humid nights, her mouth frozen open in a soundless cry of terror. According to the stories the woman can be seen walking in the garden or occasionally running across the lawn.

According to local legend yet another ghost often appears on the grounds of Liberty Hall. As the story goes, a soldier from the War of 1812 fell in love with a young cousin of the Brown family who was visiting Liberty Hall. Unfortunately the young woman did not return the soldier's affections. Heartbroken, the soldier returned to war, only to be killed during battle. For more than two centuries, the soldier's ghost has been seen peeking into the windows of the house, apparently searching for his lost love. Within a few seconds the melancholy ghost slowly turns, walks away, and vanishes from sight.

Some say the Gray Lady, the opera singer, and the heartbroken soldier continue to haunt Liberty Hall and the gardens surrounding the brick mansion. Though most people have never seen the ghostly visions, others claim their spirits remain intact, forever guarding their interests in one of Kentucky's oldest mansions.

CHAPTER 8

The Ghostly Spirits of White Hall

One of Kentucky's most famous native sons, Cassius Clay, changed his birth name to Muhammad Ali during the height of his successful boxing career. But few people realize that the parents of "The Greatest" boxer of all time chose their son's birth name in honor of Cassius Marcellus Clay, a nineteenth-century emancipationist from Kentucky.

The Cassius Clay of the 1800s was a controversial figure, both hated and loved for his firm stance against slavery. Like Ali, he was known for putting up a bold fight against his opponents. And many claim his fiery spirit continues to reign over White Hall, his palatial mansion in Madison County, Kentucky.

Born on October 19, 1810, at his family's home, Cassius was the youngest son of General Green and Sally Lewis Clay. Six of the Clay's seven children survived into adulthood. Henry Clay, Kentucky senator and four-time presidential candidate, was a first cousin of Green Clay.

Young Cassius Clay grew up surrounded by wealth and prestige. His father, one of Kentucky's earliest explorers, was a land surveyor who had accumulated hundreds of acres of land. Since printed currency was scarce in the early 1800s, land surveyors like Green Clay typically received half of the surveyed property as payment for services.

The elder Clay acquired even more real estate through land grants from the government for serving his country in the military. He not only fought Indians alongside Daniel Boone at Fort Boonesborough, he also served in the Revolutionary War and was ranked as a Brigadier General in the War of 1812. Green Clay was also known in state political circles, first serving as a court magistrate in the 1790s. In later years he served in the Kentucky legislature and the state senate.

During the 1790s Green purchased land in Madison County to build his family home. The property may have included a four-room log cabin at the edge of the property that would later serve as housing for the plantation's overseer and as an office by Cassius.

In 1798 Green began construction on a two-story brick home for his family. Bricks for the structure were fired on the site and mortared in a style known as Flemish bond. The front of the house faced north, toward the Kentucky River, and both the front and back of the home featured double doors so breezes could circulate freely through the rooms.

When the house was completed in 1799, Green named the estate Clermont. Some historians suspect that the name meant that the house was built on a "cleared" space on the "hill." Around 1810, a two-story addition was attached to one side of the building, housing the winter kitchen in the basement. Historians believe Green changed the front entrance of his home to the south side of the building at the time of the expansion to the house.

With a sharp mind for business, Green not only grew crops at Clermont, he also created businesses for selling the fruits of his labor. He owned warehouses to sell his tobacco crops, gristmills to make flour from his farm's rye and wheat, and distilleries that made spirits from the corn in his fields. He also raised and sold domestic animals, particularly Merino sheep.

As Green's enterprises expanded, service buildings were added to the Clermont estate. Barns housed livestock and crops, and other structures served as smokehouses, a blacksmith shop, and a carriage house.

To produce wealth from his land, Green depended on the labor of more than one hundred slaves. In Cassius's later years, he wrote about his father's relationship with his slaves in his book *Memoirs:*

> Now slavery was a terrible thing; but he made it as bearable as was consistent with the fact . . . There was no market for sheep in those days; and my father's object of raising large flocks was to clothe his slaves well. He always had the heaviest cloth

made for men and women. He fed and sheltered his slaves well, allowing them gardens, fowls, and bees. He provided first-class clothing, food, and shelter for his slaves, but always was rigid and exacting in discipline. Of all the men I ever knew, he most kept in view the means which influenced the end.

Though slaves were an integral part of the Clermont estate, Cassius felt strongly that slavery was unacceptable for any human. One incident that may have deeply affected Cassius as a young boy involved Mary, one of the family slaves. John Payne, a white overseer, verbally abused Mary as she cooked a meal for his family in his home. Objecting to the abuse, she riled the entire family. As they lunged to attack her, she pulled out a butcher knife and fatally stabbed Payne. Then she fled the overseer's home and ran back to the safety of Clermont.

At the murder trial in June 1820, many character witnesses testified on Mary's behalf, including the mistress of Clermont, Sally Clay. But testimonies about Mary's strong character failed to influence the jury. Mary was declared guilty of murder and sentenced to death. Only a pardon by Kentucky Governor John Adair saved her life.

After the trial Cassius continued his education at several local schools. He enrolled in Transylvania University in Lexington and later attended Yale University in Connecticut. But he never forgot the injustice of Mary's trial. He later admitted that he had enrolled at Yale with a "soul full of hatred to slavery."

While attending the prestigious university, Cassius heard a speech by the famous abolitionist William Lloyd Garrison and was deeply moved. From that moment Cassius vowed to spend the rest of his life in the fight against slavery.

By late 1828 the elder Clay's health had deteriorated. Cassius faithfully stood by his father's side until Green's death on October 31. At that time Green had become one of the largest landowners in the Commonwealth of Kentucky and perhaps the largest slaveholder, as well. In his will Green listed each of his 105 slaves by name, giving 84 slaves to his children and 1 slave to his wife. Twelve slaves were emancipated, and 8 were sold.

Green's will also bestowed his property in Madison County—some two thousand acres—and the Clermont estate to Cassius. Even though Cassius was the youngest child in the family, his older siblings had already established their own homes, and Cassius was the logical one to receive the inheritance.

In 1833 Cassius married Mary Jane Warfield, and the young couple immediately began their lives together at Clermont. Along the way Cassius renamed the family estate, changing the name to "White Hall."

As the years passed, Cassius retained his devotion to speaking out against slavery. To spread the word of his antislavery position, he published a newspaper, *The True American,* in 1845 and 1846. But his controversial opinions angered so many people that he had to place cannons and gunpowder in his printing office for personal protection.

White Hall

Cassius also launched a career as an outspoken politician. Delivering fiery speeches, he traveled throughout the country spreading his message and garnering the title of the "Lion of White Hall." At one speaking engagement, Cassius became acquainted with another Kentucky native, Abraham Lincoln. The pair formed a deep friendship, and Cassius vigorously campaigned for Lincoln in the 1860 presidential election.

After Lincoln's election, the new president appointed Cassius to serve as minister to Russia for two terms, from 1861 through 1869. By the time Clay returned from Russia, he discovered that his dream of a country without slavery had been realized. Still, for the remainder of his life, he continued to speak out for blacks and their struggle to obtain equal rights.

During Cassius's vast travels, Mary Jane remained at White Hall and supervised the construction of a massive expansion of the original Clay family home. Working with a builder and an architect, she turned the building into a palatial mansion that boasted forty-four rooms encompassing nearly ten thousand square feet of space. At the time of its completion in the 1860s, the mansion was one of the few places in the country with the modern conveniences of indoor plumbing and central heating.

Though the Clay home was opulent and luxurious, living with the headstrong, outspoken Cassius Clay was difficult, at best, for Mary Jane Clay. The marriage's breaking point occurred in 1871 when a Russian ballerina arrived at White Hall with a young boy in tow—and reportedly claimed the boy was Cassius's son. Upon the arrival of the Russians, Mary Jane packed up her belongings and left White Hall. In 1878, after forty-five years of marriage, Mary Jane and Cassius officially divorced.

In his book *Memoirs* Cassius documented many family quarrels that vilified Mary Jane. On one occasion he claimed Mary Jane had sold the family's livestock while he was traveling throughout the country and kept all of the money for herself. A review of family letters, however, indicated Mary Jane had not only been honest, but also capable and proficient, in handling her husband's finances during his travels.

In 1894 the national spotlight focused on Cassius Clay once again—but for very different reasons than political or anti-slavery issues. At age eighty-four he married Dora Richardson, whose brother was a sharecropper who worked on Cassius's land. Despite the difference in their economic status, the truly scandalous aspect of the marriage was the difference in their ages. Dora was only fifteen years old.

Cassius's second marriage lasted only a few years, ending in divorce. The Lion of White Hall lived out his remaining days at his beloved plantation until his death on July 22, 1903, at age ninety-two. After his passing, family members rented the home to tenant farmers until the mid-1960s. As the vacant mansion fell into disrepair and became the target of vandals, Cassius's descendants decided to donate the house to the state of Kentucky. Following several years of restoration, White Hall was opened to the public and designated as a state historic site in 1971.

During the first half of the twentieth century, many of White Hall's tenant farmers suspected that ghostly spirits were present inside the house and on the property. After dark the farmers observed lights floating through the grounds, appearing similar to the glow of a lantern. According to family lore, Cassius had often walked the grounds in the darkness, patrolling the estate with a lantern in hand. Was he still surveying his vast holdings long after his death?

Once the property had been abandoned, rumors started to circulate that the dilapidated mansion harbored several ghosts.

As word spread the vacant site attracted inquisitive teens and ghost hunters in search of thrills and scary encounters. And many people involved with the state's restoration of White Hall during the late 1960s have recounted stories of unexplainable incidents on the grounds.

During the mansion's renovation, security guards on overnight duty reported that they repeatedly watched the single light of a candle moving from window to window on the second floor. But each time they went into the house to investigate the mysterious light, they could never identify its origin.

According to another legend, hotheaded Cassius locked his second wife, young Dora, into a room on the second floor to keep her from running away from him. As the story goes, Dora jumped out of the window in a desperate attempt to kill herself. But a rider on horseback caught the young woman as she plummeted from the window, saving her life.

More than a decade after the house was fully restored to its former glory, a pair of park rangers saw a light in the same room where Cassius had allegedly locked his young bride. When the rangers searched the room, they could find no explanation for the light—not even light sockets. Terrified by the incident, the rangers immediately resigned from their positions.

Unexplainable lights are not the only mysteries at White Hall. Many tour guides, park rangers, and even tourists suspect that spirits of the Clay family still make their presence known in the old mansion from time to time. And the most frequently seen ghost is a dark-haired woman who may be the spirit of Mary Jane Clay.

Though the ghostly figure with dark hair usually wears black dresses, some have seen her wearing gowns in shades of blue, white, or yellow. In recent years White Hall workers have reported seeing Mary Jane's ghost on the stairway, in some of the rooms and hallways, and in front of the fireplace. On one occasion a ranger saw a woman in a black mourning gown and veil, standing in the parlor and resting her hand on a bust of Cassius Clay. At another time someone discovered a black mourning dress, along with a veil and fan, spread out on one of the beds. Was Mary Jane preparing to get dressed for a funeral?

Other ghosts of the Clay family have been seen on occasion, including the ghost of a young boy kneeling in front of the dining room fireplace with his hands outstretched, as if warming his fingers by the fire. Many suspect the boy is Elisha Clay, a son of Cassius and Mary Jane Clay, who died of typhoid fever in 1851 at age sixteen.

Another guide even witnessed the sight of Cassius with a smug smile on his face as he sat on the stairway. On another occasion a volunteer standing on the porch during a stormy evening caught a glimpse of a dark-haired man in a white shirt, standing beside her. She later learned that Cassius Clay often stood at the same place, looking out over his property in the evenings. Had the volunteer been standing beside the ghost of the Lion of White Hall?

Along with ghostly spirits, the house resounds with strange noises on occasion. One woman who worked as a housekeeper at White Hall for more than two decades reported she had heard lots of strange noises that could not be explained, particularly the sound of footsteps on the stairs when no one had been visible on the staircase. Mysterious noises have also been heard in the basement, sounding like the metal clang of pots and pans banging together. But swift inspections have never found anything out of order in the lowest level of the house. Moreover, many people have heard the sounds of furniture being moved across wood floors. After scurrying to the room and assessing the furniture placement, they have found nothing out of place.

Sounds of music have also been heard wafting through the rooms at White Hall. Violinists often played at social gatherings in the Clay mansion during the 1800s, and their haunting refrains can still be heard from time to time. During the early 1980s, for instance, a group of women spent the night at White Hall. Around two o'clock in the morning, the women were awakened by soft violin music drifting up the stairs. As they crept down the staircase to investigate the sounds, the music abruptly ended. The women stopped in their tracks, remembering that the only violin in the house had no strings.

When White Hall was abandoned during the mid-1960s, one woman exploring the dilapidated mansion heard someone in the house playing a portion of Beethoven's Third Symphony on the piano. Laura Clay, one of the Clay children, often played an 1859 Steinway piano that has since been returned to the White Hall ballroom. One morning in the late 1990s, a tour guide arrived early to unlock the mansion for the day's tours. Preparing to step inside the house, she heard piano music coming from the direction of the ballroom. However, the piano had not yet been restored and was incapable of producing any melodic tunes. Had Laura Clay returned to practice for her piano lessons? Since that time some tour guides and groups claim they have heard random piano notes resounding from the ballroom. Even the sounds of a music box have been heard on two separate occasions within a period of two days. But no music boxes are present in the house.

Inexplicable scents waft through the house, as well. Often the strong smell of pipe smoke permeates the ballroom or dining room and then suddenly disappears without a trace. On one occasion a guide noted the distinct odor of burning candles in the dining room. Since park policies prohibit burning candles in the historic house, the guide asked a friend to help her investigate the smell. But as she and her friend entered the dining room, the scent had mysteriously vanished.

The most common unexplainable odor at White Hall is the scent of perfume at the top of the staircase. One guide insisted she smelled an old-fashioned fragrance similar to a flowery lemon scent. Concentrated in one area, the scent almost overpowered her. When she stepped away from the staircase and entered the hallway, however, she could no longer detect the odor.

Muffled voices have also been heard throughout the house. Guides have heard a voice calling out to them from another room. But once they head in the direction of the voice, no one can be found. More than one tour group has heard several people arguing on the third floor. Although they could not understand what the voices were saying, they could detect both men's and women's voices. On another day three tour guides heard muffled voices coming from the basement. To make sure the intruders could not escape, each guide guarded separate entrances to the basement. But the voices suddenly disappeared, and the guides found no trace of any humans in the lowest level of the house.

White Hall employees have insisted that the mansion's ghostly spirits can be playful at times. They rattle doorknobs and disappear as soon as someone opens the door. They love to turn on lights that have been turned off. And no one can explain how, without the help of breezes from open windows, they rattle the crystal sconces in the hallway or swing the black ropes that block certain areas of the mansion from visitors.

Today White Hall has earned the reputation of being one of Kentucky's most famous haunted houses. Undoubtedly the strong-willed spirit of Cassius M. Clay has remained at the palatial mansion, determined to keep controversy alive and well for future generations at the magnificent estate.

CHAPTER 9

Where Is Daniel Boone Buried?

With his frontier adventures in the exploration and settlement of the area now known as Kentucky, Daniel Boone became one of America's first folk heroes. Revered for his bravery and leadership, Boone became a living legend in his own time. But his death brought controversy over his rightful burial place—and ignited a battle between two states that continues to this day.

Two states claim to hold the remains of Daniel Boone: Missouri, the site of his death, and Kentucky, the state that supposedly transferred his remains from Missouri for reburial. So is Daniel Boone buried in Kentucky or Missouri? The mystery is fitting for a man who traversed the American frontier but was rarely able to call the land he crossed over his home without some sort of dispute.

Daniel Boone was born on November 2, 1734, in Berks County (now Montgomery), Pennsylvania. His Quaker parents, Squire and Sarah, were eventually forced to flee Pennsylvania when Squire allowed his son Israel to marry a non-Quaker. Teenager Daniel relocated with his family to Yadkin Valley, North Carolina, in 1752. With little formal schooling beyond the three R's, he honed his hunting and trapping skills alongside other hunters and Native Americans. These relationships proved fruitful for Boone in his later adventures.

In 1756 Boone married Rebecca Bryan, the daughter of another prominent family of settlers. Legend notes the pair met when Boone was hunting one night and mistakenly thought she was a bear as she tended her father's livestock. However, the pair actually met at a family wedding. Boone's sister Mary married William Bryan, who later explored Kentucky with his three brothers and established Bryan Station settlement. The marriages between the Boones and Bryans cemented the clans as the founding families in early Kentucky exploration. Daniel and Rebecca Boone produced ten children; Mary and William Bryan had nine.

During the early years of his marriage, Boone was often away from home, fighting the Cherokees during the French and Indian Wars. When the war wound down in 1763, Boone returned home but could not settle into the life of a farmer or planter. Companies of hunters from Pennsylvania, Virginia, and North Carolina circulated stories of the game in the valleys along and west of the Tennessee River, luring Boone into the wilderness. He pursued long hunting, which gave him the freedom to explore the headwaters of the Holston and Cumberland Rivers.

Long hunts could last a year or more, suiting Boone's passion for adventure. After Cherokees raided Yadkin Valley, Boone even explored as far south as Pensacola, Florida. His wife, however, dissuaded him from settling there.

Boone skirted the Kentucky landscape as early as 1767 during a hunting expedition with his brother Squire. John Finley, an Indian trader and acquaintance, had lured the brothers to the area with tales of grand picturesque mountains, sheltered valleys, rich canebrakes, and bountiful game. With the financial support of Judge Richard Henderson of North Carolina, Boone set out on his first official expedition into Kentucky in May 1769. Along with five companions Boone and his group started the hunting and trapping expedition in the Cumberland Gap and eventually made their way to Pilot Knob in Powell County. In December the party split into two smaller groups, but this decision proved fateful. Shawnees captured all the men and eventually killed everyone but Boone, who managed to escape with the help of Squire.

In spite of the conflicts with Indians, the appeal of the land enticed Boone to move his family to Kentucky in 1773, along with five other families. After an Indian attack killed many settlers, including Boone's oldest son James, the majority of the settlers were scared off and returned to their former homes. The following year Captain Boone fought valiantly for Lord Dunsmore who, in turn, solicited Boone to go to the Falls of the Ohio and survey the area for settlement.

On March 17, 1775, Colonel Richard Henderson signed the Treaty of Sycamore Shoals with the Cherokees, offering two thousand pounds and trading goods valued at eight thousand pounds, while securing twenty million acres between the Ohio, Kentucky, and Cumberland Rivers for the Transylvania Land Company. Henderson hired explorers, such as Boone, to scout the territory and establish civil relationships with the Indian tribes, hoping to obtain western land settlements and start a fourteenth colony. Boone had built a solid reputation for negotiating with the Cherokees as a company agent, so his profile stimulated sales for the company's venture.

No sooner had the treaty terms been signed than Henderson commissioned Boone to build a road into the region and establish Kentucky's second settlement. By April 1775 Boone had successfully erected Fort Boonesborough on the banks of the Kentucky River; he had sent for his family by September.

The Revolutionary War on the eastern seaboard mirrored the violence between the Native Americans and the pioneer settlers. By 1776 the British had attempted to thwart settlers from moving west by sealing its borders around Virginia. Moreover, the Virginia legislature nullified the Transylvania Company's land claims stemming from the Treaty of Sycamore Shoals and made the land a county of Virginia. The settlers battled dual fronts: the British who tried in vain to thwart westward migration without the manpower to protect or profit from the land, and the Indians who wanted to reclaim their lands. Boone's daughter Jemima and two other women were captured by a Shawnee war party in July 1776, resulting in a daring rescue by Boone and several Boonesborough men two days later.

In early February 1778, as Boone and thirty men went to a nearby salt lick to replenish their exhausted salt supply, they were ambushed by Shawnees led by Chief Black Fish. Forced into captivity, Boone and his party observed the Shawnee culture, were given Indian names, and, most important, obtained information that the Shawnees were going to attack Fort Boonesborough. Ironically, during his five-month captivity, Boone gained the trust of Black Fish and eventually became the chief's adopted son. Boone's ease in relating to Native Americans may have been further helped by the fact that he dressed like them, spiking up his hair with bear grease and wrapping himself in black deerskins.

During a rare solo hunting trip, Boone ran away on horseback with a small supply of armaments. Arriving in Fort Boonesborough on June 16, 1778, he was greeted with great skepticism. First, the fort commanders admonished Boone for taking thirty men from the fort and leaving it vulnerable to defense. Then, Boone had to defend his character. A few members of Boone's salt-gathering party, who had escaped Shawnee captivity before Boone had, circulated a story that Boone had offered to surrender Boonesborough with safe conveyance of its settlers to Detroit. In truth Boone had used this tactic as a shrewd strategy to turn British attention away from ill-equipped Boonesborough.

Even though the accusations against him were not accurate, Boone had little time to defend himself from rumors of treason. Midmorning September 7, 1778, Boone and his scouts watched four hundred Shawnees come down the north side of the Kentucky River. And the Shawnees were not alone. Along with them came the British-backed French-Canadian Lieutenant Antoine de Quindre and his company of Detroit militia, as well as an assemblage of Wyandots, Cherokees, Miamis, Delawares, and Mingoes.

Chief Black Fish led the Shawnees. As the Indians drew near to Boone and his men, Black Fish's interpreter, Pompey, revealed de Quindre's terms for surrender, telling Boone to take the terms back to Fort Boonesborough for consideration. The French and Native Americans released Boone and his scouts, but as soon as Boone reached the fort, he and the fort commanders quickly assessed its defenses. As four hundred Indians and French closed in around Boonesborough's perimeter, Chief Black Fish waited to hear a response from the fort. When none was forthcoming after one day, he sent word to the fort that he had a new reason for surrender: The settlers must leave Kentucky, because they were trespassing on Shawnee territory.

Boone and his companions refused to leave, reminding Black Fish of conditions forfeited by the Sycamore Shoals Treaty. Black Fish countered with another set of conditions: The Ohio River would act as the boundary between the two parties and could not be crossed by either side for any malicious purposes.

Boone and the settlers realized there would be no more stalling and the terms of this agreement were better than the first. But as both parties signed the document, the Indians seized Boone and his companions. Somehow the men managed to break free and ran back to the fort.

The siege continued for a week, until the Indians made a final, unsuccessful attempt to take the fort. During the siege only two settlers were killed and four were wounded. When the settlers arose one morning to find the enemy had disappeared, they wondered if they were being tricked in an attempt by the Indians to lure them out of the fort. Eventually, however, the settlers felt safe enough to leave the compound. Exonerated from treason charges, Boone was eventually promoted to the rank of major for his service.

Boone's role during the American Revolution became settlement protector rather than freedom fighter. He was part of the last battle in the Revolutionary War, the Battle of Blue Licks, in 1782. His role as lieutenant colonel of one of two Kentucky militia forces proved costly when he saw his son Israel shot and killed during the siege. Boone was forever riddled with guilt about his son's death, knowing it had been his own decision to defend a site that was later ambushed.

When Kentucky became the fifteenth state admitted to the Union in 1792, litigation ensued over the rightful title to settler land. Boone lost thousands of acres when Virginia incorporated the region assumed under the Transylvania Company after the Revolution. He failed to comply with the preemption requirements, possibly the result of failing to carefully read and understand the terms. Not only was Boone landless, he was also marred by lawsuits filed by individuals who claimed he had erroneously surveyed land, which left the property open to counter claims.

The start of the nineteenth century did not appear to be promising for the debt-ridden Boone, who complained Kentucky was becoming too crowded. Between 1795 and 1799 Boone and his wife moved to Spanish-owned Missouri, enticed by a land grant of eighty-five hundred acres forty-five miles north of St. Louis. Spain was thrilled to attract such a famous settler and further commissioned Boone as a magistrate of the Femme Osage District (St. Charles County) in 1800. Boone's notoriety even drew curiosity seekers, including painter Chester Harding, who completed a portrait of Boone at age eighty-six. While Boone sat for his portrait, Harding asked if he had ever gotten lost, especially without a compass. Boone replied, "I can't say as ever I was lost, but I was bewildered once for three days."

Ironically Boone lost his Missouri acreage after he failed to cultivate the land, a stipulation from the federal government's Louisiana Purchase from Spain. Redemption occurred in 1814 when Kentucky senators petitioned Congress to grant Boone one tenth of his original holdings.

Boone spent his later years hunting and exploring virgin lands of the Missouri territory north and west of St. Louis with his sons and grandsons. The Boones lived their remaining years with their children until Rebecca's death on March 18, 1813. Rebecca was buried on the Bryan family farm on Tuque Creek.

Boone's last hunting trip occurred in 1816 before he fell victim to on-again-off-again illness and fever and started to lose his hearing and sight. After one particular meal of his favorite dish, sweet potatoes, Boone told his daughter he was suffering from an acute burning sensation resonant with either a heart attack or indigestion. Refusing medication, Boone died before sunrise on September 26, 1820, surrounded by his large progeny. Out of respect for Boone's passing, the Constitutional Convention meeting in St. Louis required members to wear a badge of mourning for thirty days.

Nathan Boone reported his father's funeral was fitting for an unpretentious man. The services took place at the home of Jemima and Flanders Callaway, with neither military nor Masonic honors, even though Boone had been a member of both organizations. The Baptist funeral conducted by Reverend James Craig, Nathan's son-in-law, created a large entourage. Nathan noted his father's remains were buried next to his mother's plot, a mile from the Missouri River. Nathan's version of the location of Boone's body would eventually conflict with the recollections of other funeral attendees.

Although Boone wished to be buried next to his wife, the burial plot next to Rebecca Boone's plot was already taken. As a result his family buried him in a plot located at the foot of

Daniel Boone's grave and monument in Frankfort, Kentucky is a tiered white
monument with square sides surrounded by a high iron fence.
On the largest part of the monument is a panel carved with what looks like
Boone fighting with another man who is raising a tomahawk.

Rebecca's grave. Since most graves of the day were unmarked,
Boone's great niece contracted Captain John Wyatt to erect
two stone slabs over the graves of Daniel and Rebecca Boone in
1835. Over the course of time, the markers became difficult to
distinguish, and the graves became unkempt among the others
in the cemetery. Moreover, several slaves retained by the Boone
offspring were also buried in the graveyard.

During an 1840 celebration at Boonesborough, Kentuckians proposed raising a statue for Boone to honor his legacy. But

the proposal took another turn when the Kentucky legislature passed a resolution authorizing the relocation of Boone's remains to the state capital in Frankfort. Aside from honoring one of the state's founding fathers, state officials also hoped the plot would boost the city's tourism industry. A Kentucky contingency wrote a letter to Nathan Boone requesting permission to remove Daniel Boone's remains and bring them back to Kentucky where "if from the other world the Boones could speak, [they] would prefer being buried in Kentucky to any part of the globe." Upon hearing Kentucky's request, Missouri officials quickly appropriated five hundred dollars to erect a monument over Boone's Tuque Creek grave.

The Kentucky contingency then contacted Boone's elderly nephew William Linville Boone, who was still living in Kentucky, and asked him to go to Missouri and contact Boone's heirs. The enticement was a ten thousand dollar appropriation to build a stately monument honoring Boone. Finally, in 1945, traveling by way of the steamer *Daniel Boone,* the Kentucky contingency—made up of William L. Boone, Thomas Crittenden, and Jacob Swiggert—reached Missouri and sought Daniel Boone's sole surviving son, Nathan. But Nathan was out of town, so William pressed the two daughters of Daniel's predeceased son Jesse for their consent. Once the women gave their consent, the Kentuckians proceeded to the Bryan farm graveyard. But the owner, Harvey Griswold, did not approve of the removal of the bodies, having paid a large sum for the farm with the knowledge that Boone's remains were interred on the property. Showing the heirs' consent, the Kentucky contingency assured Griswold that the Frankfort cemetery would compensate him for his property's loss of value.

As three black men hired by the Kentucky contingency dug up the graves, a crowd of thirty to forty assorted Boones, Bryans, and neighbors circulated around the gravesite. If any family members opposed the exhumation, they remained silent. The St. Louis press quoted family members who agreed to the exhumation as long as Kentucky upheld its end of the bargain and rightfully honored Boone. As the men brought up the remains, the coffins deteriorated under the spade of the shovel. Bones crumbled when the men loaded the remains, and several locals picked up bits of bone and teeth to keep as relics.

On September 13, 1845, Frankfort residents lined the streets as a parade led by a hearse and four white horses proceeded from the Capitol building, across the Kentucky River, and up the hill to the Frankfort Cemetery. At the gravesite, Senator John J. Crittenden gave a luminous eulogy on behalf of Boone. Missing amid the pomp and circumstance was the proposed monument, which was not erected until 1860, after the state legislature appropriated two thousand dollars for its creation. However, the monument had to be rebuilt two years later, after Union soldiers defaced it during the Civil War.

Missourians resented the disinterment. An 1888 editorial in the *St. Louis Globe-Democrat* chided that Boone's grave was "desecrated to gratify a spasm of Kentucky pride . . . for which Missouri should never forgive." According to rumors, Boone's Missouri heirs were so upset by the move that they didn't inform the grave diggers of Boone's true location and allowed Rebecca's bones to be carried off along with bones belonging to someone else. Since the grave markers for Daniel and Rebecca had been mistakenly placed side-by-side, even though Daniel was supposed to have been buried at the foot of Rebecca's plot, it was not unlikely that his remains lay undisturbed.

More than 160 years after Boone's death, a Kentucky anthropologist made a notable observation about the bones that had been transferred from the Missouri graveyard in 1845. On the night before Daniel Boone's reburial in Kentucky, Reverend Phillip Slater Fall made a plaster cast of Boone's skull. In 1983, Dr. David Wolf, Kentucky's state forensic anthropologist, examined the cast at the Kentucky Historical Society. Wolf noted that the cast resembled the skull of an African American with a round forehead that lacked the predominant slope of a typical Caucasian male skull. "The general shape of the brow ridges are more black than white; the occipital bone is more pronounced, protruding or bun-shaped, which is a black feature," noted Wolf. He also observed that the indentation of the frontal bone, the postorbital construction, tended to mirror an African American more than a Caucasian male. Moreover Wolf contended that the body buried in Frankfort Cemetery was large and robust, a sharp contrast to Boone's frame of five feet, eight or nine inches that had been documented by his brother-in-law Daniel Bryan.

Wolf's announcement sent shockwaves throughout the state and reached national newspapers, including the *New York Times.* Though Wolf admitted the casting was poor, it was the only specimen available for examination. Without examining more of Boone's remains, Wolf would have difficulty determining whether or not the cast was of the famed American pioneer. Frankfort officials refuted Wolf's results and insisted the pioneer's remains lay in Frankfort.

More familiar with examining human bones for criminal cases or to determine unidentified remains, Wolf planned to examine the rest of the skeletal remains buried in Frankfort Cemetery to determine the race of the person. However, Wolf himself understood that Boone's original Missouri burial grounds were deteriorating, as evidenced by disintegrating coffins and crumbling bones. Even Boone's Kentucky burial plot had been tampered with on at least one occasion in the 138 years since the interred remains had been moved from Missouri.

The matter of Daniel Boone's final resting place again created controversy in 1987. Mockingly, Missouri officials requested that Kentucky return Rebecca's remains to lie next to Daniel Boone's remains in Missouri. The Warren County government petitioned John Ashcroft, then-governor of Missouri, to issue a proclamation declaring Boone's bones had never left the state. The move would solidify the old Bryan farm to be a Daniel

Boone tourist site. Kentucky officials even considered moving Boone's Frankfort remains to Boonesborough State Park to bolster its own tourism. However, the Kentucky state legislature vetoed this idea. No matter where his final resting place, both sites sit on a precipice overlooking river vistas, a sight similar to what Boone himself often observed during the course of his life.

CHAPTER 10

The Curse of Anne Mitchell

John Bell Hood, one of Kentucky's most famous native sons, served as a brilliant general in the Confederate Army. Yet a series of devastating tragedies in General Hood's life overshadowed his remarkable military career. Was the potency of a Kentucky woman's dying curse the reason for his misfortunes?

Raised in Montgomery County, Kentucky, John lived near the little town of Mount Sterling. His father, Dr. John W. Hood, was a physician who operated a large farm and a school for aspiring doctors. Beautiful Anne Mitchell, who was about the same age as the younger John, lived nearby. Growing up in such close proximity to each other, John and Anne must have known each other for most of their lives.

In the summer of 1849, eighteen-year-old John entered West Point Military Academy. On his first leave of absence from the academy, John returned home to discover that the girl next door had blossomed into a breathtaking beauty. A striking brunette in her late teens who often wore shimmering gray gowns to highlight the color of her lustrous eyes, Anne had become known throughout the region as "the belle of Central Kentucky." With her reputation of being gentle and sweet, numerous suitors called at her door. But it was John Bell Hood, the tall, blond cadet with broad shoulders, who captured her heart.

John and Anne often took evening walks through the gardens of the Hood home, their favorite meeting place, and spent time together sitting on a loveseat that overlooked the orchards of the Hood farm.

According to family lore, another young man also became interested in Anne about the same time. Some versions of the story contend the man's name was Thomas Anderson, while other accounts refer to him only as "Mr. Anderson." No matter his given name, however, Anne did not care for him. Though she could hardly ignore his frequent visits to the Mitchell home—supposedly to see her brothers—she did not encourage his attentions. But he boldly pursued her, promising to build a home for her on property that adjoined her family's land.

The young man's wealth and persistence must have impressed Anne's family, who pressured her to accept his proposal of marriage. Caving into their demands, Anne agreed to marry her suitor only if she could write a letter to John, who had returned to West Point. In her letter, she promised to love John throughout eternity and vowed she would "walk the garden path" by his side, "whether in this world or the next."

General John Bell Hood

LIBRARY OF CONGRESS

As soon as John received the letter, he headed home to Kentucky. He somehow managed to relay a message to Anne, instructing her to slip out of the house after dark on a certain evening and meet him at a location near her home. He promised to bring an extra horse with him, saddled for her, and they would ride off together and secretly elope.

Eager to escape her pending marriage and spend the rest of her life with John, Anne followed his directions. But as soon as she had slipped out of the house, a slave girl discovered that Anne was missing from her bed. The girl quickly informed the family. Anne's father and brothers immediately saddled their horses and set out to find her.

The Mitchell men caught up with the couple just as John was helping Anne onto her horse, and they forced her to return home with them. She was locked in her room to prevent another secret escape.

Anne remained behind locked doors until her wedding day. She dutifully exchanged wedding vows with Anderson, but the bride could not hide her bitterness over the forced marriage. Despite her new husband's love, adoration, and wealth, Anne could not forgive her family for denying her the love of John Hood. After the wedding she secluded herself in her old room in the Mitchell home, remaining depressed and forlorn. Not even the news of her pregnancy could lift her spirits. She banished her husband from her bedchambers and refused to speak to the rest of the family.

Not until the birth of her son Corwin did Anne finally speak again. Her words evoked an ominous tone throughout the household as she cursed "all who had any part in making me marry Mr. Anderson when my heart will always belong to John Bell Hood."

A few hours after Anne had spoken those fateful words, thunder rumbled through the afternoon skies over Mount

Sterling, and an eerie darkness enveloped the Mitchell home. Then a bolt of lightning struck the corner of the house that contained Anne's room. That portion of the brick structure collapsed, killing three people in the home: Anne, one of her brothers who had pressured her into marrying Mr. Anderson, and the slave girl who had prevented Anne's elopement. Ironically, no other structures in the area were damaged by the sudden storm.

With three people dead within hours of Anne's damning curse on all who had played a role in separating her from the love of her life, the story of the curse spread like wildfire. And years later Anne continued to make her presence known to her own son. As a young boy Corwin reportedly saw his mother walking along the garden path near Hood's home. Since Anne had died only a few hours after Corwin's birth, the young boy could not have had any memories of her physical appearance. But his descriptions of the woman who had been walking through the flowery pathway bore a remarkable similarity to the features of his own mother.

As Anderson listened to his son's descriptions of the young woman in the garden, a sinking feeling swept through him. Had Anne's ghost appeared to remind everyone that her curse on the family continued?

When the winds of war swept through the country, Anderson enlisted in the Confederate Army. Some historical accounts contend that he enlisted in a Texas regiment, which was later commanded by General John Bell Hood. Most versions say

Anderson was officially declared as missing in action shortly after reporting for military duty, and any further records of him have never been found.

Like his father, Corwin became a wealthy Kentucky land baron. By 1880 he had two young sons, Isaac and English Anderson. Isaac, the younger son, was known throughout the community for his generosity and kind, gentle spirit.

English, however, garnered a much different reputation. Neighbors in Mount Sterling could not ignore the violent temper of the disgruntled young man. In 1891 English confronted the family cook in the kitchen, enraged that his potatoes were undercooked. Though the cook apologized, the unforgiving English reached for a carving knife and stabbed him to death. The murder led to a trial, but the jury ruled in favor of the son of a wealthy landowner, determining English had acted in self-defense.

But English's temper continued to rule his thoughts and actions. Soon after the trial, Isaac was surveying the family's vast property holdings, riding on horseback, when English confronted him. A heated argument ensued between the brothers. One version of the story claims that English cursed his brother, taking on a woman's voice that claimed the Anderson family had always tried to control the lives of others.

English then picked up a brick and hurled it at Isaac's head. The force of the blow knocked Isaac from his horse, instantly killing him. Frightened farmhands rushed to the Anderson home to inform their master of the death of his younger son. Though Corwin requested to see his son's body, the shock of Isaac's murder was too much to bear. Before he could leave the house, Corwin died of a heart attack.

After the deaths of his brother and father, English's violence and rage blossomed unchecked. He seemed bent on destroying the Anderson family and fortune. Most people attributed English's rage to the curse that his grandmother had uttered decades earlier. In 1901 English had a son of his own, Judson, but not even fatherhood could quell his antisocial behavior.

The residents of Mount Sterling believed English was the manifestation of the hatred left behind by his mother, and they feared both Anne's curse and English's unchecked temper. Eventually, English killed a man in a knife fight and then beat to death a young boy who was working on his farm. In revenge, a group of other farm workers stoned English to death.

For the next three decades, Judson, Anne's great-grandson, lived on the Anderson property. Some say he was haunted by dreams and visions of Anne's ghost moving through the halls of the house and garden paths that separated the neighboring properties. By the 1940s he could no longer cope with the torment. Naked and carrying a pistol, Judson waded waist-deep into one of the ponds that decorated the garden path. He fired a single shot into his temple, ending the Anderson legacy.

Though Anne's malicious curse devastated the lives of her family, her lingering spirit reflected the gentle, graceful girl who had once been known as the belle of Central Kentucky. Those who reported seeing her ghost wandering through the gardens of the Mitchell and Hood properties said she possessed a quiet, thoughtful nature. Aside from the frightening experience of encountering a ghost, eyewitnesses contended that her gentle presence was not intimidating at all.

One former slave claimed to have seen Anne promenading through the gardens on several occasions. She would stop, stare at the old woman, and then vanish. And a tenant of one of the properties reported that he had been awakened from a deep sleep, sensing someone was in the room. He sat up, seeing a woman in a filmy dress of shimmering gray—Anne's favorite color—bathed in moonlight shining through the windows. She looked so real to him, standing there at the foot of his bed, that the man was stunned when she suddenly disappeared into thin air.

As the years progressed, the effects of Anne's curse seemed to wreak havoc on the lives of subsequent residents of the Hood property. One owner killed himself, while a second owner attempted to commit suicide over a disastrous love affair.

Despite Anne's love for John Bell Hood, some say that he, too, became an unintentional victim of her curse. Did her restless spirit pass along the effects of the curse to the very man she loved? After his separation from Anne, Hood's life was plagued with failures and tragedies.

Some versions of the story declare that Hood faithfully wrote to Anne during his travels throughout the Civil War, unaware of her death after their parting. Other accounts suggest that he devoted himself to military service and forgot about the Kentucky belle after he graduated from West Point. Serving in a Texas regiment under the command of Lieutenant Colonel Robert E. Lee, Hood may have listened to his commander's advice against "forming a permanent attachment for some of these country lasses." At one point, the commander warned his solders, "Never marry unless you can do so into a family which will enable your children to feel proud of both sides of the house."

Hood eventually became a commander in the Texas unit, which was considered to be one of the strongest in the Confederate Army, and his career began to flourish. With his heroic actions, Hood gained the reputation of a strong leader. Instead of leading his soldiers from the sidelines, he always stepped forward and led his own troops into battle. By placing himself at the forefront of battles, however, he paid a physical price for his bravery. While leading the charge of his division at Gettysburg, he lost one of his arms. And after taking the lead of his troops at the bloody battle of Chickamauga, Hood suffered injuries to his leg, which later had to be amputated.

At the height of his career—despite having only one arm and one leg—Hood was promoted to the rank of full general. When he assumed command of the western army, he was only thirty-three years old. As soon as his career reached its peak, however, he encountered a series of devastating losses in battle.

In charge of the defense of Atlanta, Hood and his men were driven out of the city as Union General William T. Sherman charged through Georgia and burned the capital city during his march to the sea. At the Battle of Nashville in the winter of 1864, Hood suffered another disgrace when Union troops practically destroyed the Army of Tennessee, which was under his command. No other Confederate general had suffered a worse defeat.

At the close of the war, Hood settled in New Orleans and attempted to run a cotton brokerage. He fell in love and married a local woman, Anna Hennen. Their marriage produced ten children, including three sets of twins. But Hood could not escape further tragedies in his life. His business failed to thrive and eventually went bankrupt. Then, thirty years after his botched attempt to elope with Anne Mitchell, John contracted yellow fever in the epidemic of 1879. He died from the disease, along with his wife, leaving ten destitute orphans.

Military historians have often portrayed John Bell Hood as a womanizer with a penchant for beautiful ladies. The legend of Anne's curse and the romantic story of Hood's relationship with her, no doubt, influenced the depiction.

Though the story of the forbidden courtship and the devastating effects of Anne's curse have been handed down from generation to generation, one descendent of the Anderson family adamantly insisted that the story was not true. After a 1948 article about Anne's curse appeared in *Life* magazine, Sidney

Hart Anderson filed a $275,000 lawsuit against the publication for libel. The magazine eventually settled the lawsuit, paying an undisclosed sum to the Anderson descendent.

Still, local legends contend that the tragedies resulting from the curse of Anne Mitchell were much more than coincidence. In the Anderson home, family members were plagued with strange and violent deaths, while tragedy after tragedy marred John Bell Hood's life—possibly caused by the lingering anger of a woman whose family denied her a chance at true love.

CHAPTER 11

Edgar Cayce: The Sleeping Prophet

In 1909, F. O. Putnam's rambunctious twenty-one-month-old son began suffering a high fever and spasmodic jerking. Dizzy spells further complicated the boy's condition. Over a period of two weeks, Putnam and his wife enlisted a local Little Rock, Arkansas, physician to watch the child around the clock. After the doctor suppressed the boy's fever, Putnam assumed his son was on the mend and resumed his business travel. However, the boy began to experience swelling and pain in his legs every time he attempted to walk. Doctors thought the child had a joint infection in his knees and recommended casts.

While on business in Indiana, Putnam received correspondence from his wife in Arkansas that their son's condition had worsened. Putnam scribed a quick letter, asking for Edgar Cayce to conduct a psychic reading for his son. Putnam expressly asked Cayce to send the diagnosis to his wife in Arkansas. Although Cayce lived in Alabama, he psychically provided a description of the problem and prescribed a course of treatment. Cayce concluded the child was experiencing an enlarged liver with an excess of bile, bowel obstruction, poor circulation, and kidney malfunction, limiting his ability to walk. Cayce requested Mrs. Putnam take her child to Bowling Green, Kentucky, osteopath T. W. Posey.

Posey treated the Putnam boy under Cayce's direction. Cayce's treatment plan for the child called for healing vibrations to stimulate the nervous system and digestive tract. Healing vibrations ranged from castor oil applications to a radial appliance that passed electrical stimulants through the body. After a two-month rehabilitation, Posey declared the child cured of his affliction. Putnam acknowledged in a sworn affidavit to a Boston research society that Cayce had cured his son, who had since grown to be a healthy toddler.

By 1910 Cayce's fame as a psychic healer was beginning to spread outside of his native Kentucky. Born in 1877 in Hopkinsville, Cayce was one of five children of a local farmer and businessman. Somewhat of a free spirit and independent child, Cayce often perplexed his parents by playing with imaginary playmates. Although his parents attributed his lively imagination to a stage of development, Cayce believed these imaginary friends to be real. Even in adulthood he recalled that he was visited by spirits who frightened or threatened him.

When Cayce's grandparents came to live with his family, he developed a close bond with his grandfather Tom. The pair often spent time fishing, curing tobacco, and riding horses. After a horse accident tragically killed Tom, Cayce's parents found the four-year-old boy in the tobacco barn, conversing with his dead grandfather.

His psychic powers have been attributed to an accident at the tender age of three. He fell from a fence post onto a board, directly hitting his head on a nail and puncturing his cranium. Having seen the fall, his father picked him up and removed the nail while his mother immediately applied turpentine, a popular treatment of the day, to the wound.

Although he recovered from the trauma, psychic research-ers have alluded that psychic abilities are often attributed to severe blows to the head that may alter pituitary or pineal glands. Cayce never attributed the accident to his powers, believing his psychic ability was the handiwork of God.

Cayce was raised as a Disciple of Christ, concentrating most of his efforts in studying the Bible. Old Testament stories highlighting paranormal or supernatural phenomena, including Moses and Pharaoh's magicians, captured the boy's attention. By age twelve he claimed to have read the Bible twelve times.

One of Cayce's most pronounced visions occurred when a female angel appeared before the thirteen-year-old in a secluded spot in the woods. When the angel asked what he wanted most, he responded he wanted to help others. The apparition rankled Cayce so much that he began to have trouble sleeping at night and concentrating in school. Never a strong student, he often had difficulty with his homework. One late night as he tried to study his spelling, his father Tom thought a rest would help clear the boy's mind. When Tom went to the kitchen and returned, he saw his son had fallen asleep atop his textbook. When he awoke, he recited everything in the book. Cayce pinpointed this incident as the origin for his method of retaining knowledge. He could sleep on any textbook and recite the text word for word after awakening. He carried this technique into adulthood by lying down and entering a self-induced sleep state. In later years this practice earned him the name of the "sleeping prophet."

Cayce's transient young adulthood started when he left school at age sixteen to help on his grandmother's farm. Farming disinterested him, so he got a job in a bookstore, where he met his future wife, Gertrude. Still young and unsure of his ambitions, Cayce decided to delay marriage to Gertrude and venture into photography and insurance. On one particular insurance sales trip in 1900, Cayce came down with severe laryngitis. The condition lingered for ten months, forcing him to quit his job and return to both Gertrude and photography. Cayce's family took him for a private consultation with a traveling hypnotist, Hart the Laugh King. As soon as King hypnotized him, Cayce regained his voice. However, once the hypnosis wore off, his voice disappeared again.

Cayce then turned to a local hypnotist, Al Layne, for help. Layne hypnotized him, but then Cayce took over the hypnosis and started a reading on him! When Cayce awoke from Layne's hypnosis, his voice was permanently restored. This incident on March 31, 1901, marked Cayce's first successful reading.

Impressed by the episode, Layne asked Cayce to return the favor by ridding him of his stomach ailments. Layne, who had received his osteopathic training through a mail-order degree, had been recently asked by the local Hopkinsville medical community to cease his osteopathy operation. Either Layne viewed Cayce as possible substantiation for continuing his practice, or he wanted to further validate Cayce's clairvoyance. Whatever the case, the pair formed a unique partnership: Cayce would provide a diagnosis and Layne would interpret Cayce's suggested remedy.

One of Cayce's first patients was five-year-old Aimee Dietrich, who had suffered from convulsions for two years. Cayce recommended osteopathic therapy for the girl, which was conducted by Layne. Within three months Aimee was fully healed. But just as Cayce's notoriety began to circulate, the partnership unraveled. In 1903 Cayce married Gertrude, started a family, and opened a new photography studio in Bowling Green; Layne moved to Franklin to start the Southern School of Osteopathy.

Hypnosis, the state in which an individual becomes responsive to suggestions, dates back to the 1780s with the work of Austrian physician Anton Mesmer. The physician believed the nervous system was magnetized, just like the earth, and referred to this phenomenon as "animal magnetism." Mesmer attracted a large European following that attributed animal magnetism—or mesmerism, as it was popularly called—as a cure for all physical and mental ailments. A vast body of literature on mesmerism made its way from Europe to the United States, expanding on the relationship between clairvoyance and telepathy, personal power and rejuvenation.

Mesmerists believed the field opened a window into human physiology. Mesmerist writers attempted to marry the elements of science (magnetism, electricity, and force) with theology (mind, body, and spirit). As a result, mesmerism adopted both a religious and metaphysical following during the late nineteenth century. Traveling clairvoyance, in which one can see things but not interact nor interfere, became a common practice during this time. Fifty years prior to Cayce, for instance, Andrew Jackson Davis, dubbed the "Poughkeepsie Seer," was able to read closed books, diagnose illness, and prescribe treatment.

During the 1840s British physicians—notably James Esdaile and John Eliotson—began to explore hypnosis for pain management and pain reduction during surgery. Scottish surgeon James Braid developed more precise techniques for hypnosis by differentiating the neuromuscular processes that occur in a patient during the induction of a hypnotic trance. Subsequent physicians in the nineteenth century theorized a patient's will was paralyzed during a hypnotic trance and that unconscious mental processes could be observed.

After parting ways with Al Layne, Cayce handed over Layne's role to a trained doctor, John Blackburn. In 1906 Blackburn persuaded Cayce to give a public reading before the

Bowling Green E.Q.B. Literary Club attended by a handful of local doctors. When Cayce went into his trance, doctors tested Cayce's response to external stimuli to determine whether his hypnosis was genuine. One poked him with a hatpin, while another cut the nail from his left forefinger. Upon waking up, Cayce vowed to never be tested under any controlled conditions by doctors or scientists. The experience severed both the partnership with Blackburn as well as Cayce's interest in substantiating his powers before any established medical community.

Up until this point Cayce had continued his career as a photographer, because he was unsure if his psychic powers were reliable enough to provide for his family. Moreover, he doubted if God would approve of him healing people in this way. However, several misfortunes struck in 1909 that prompted him to rethink his career path. After two fires destroyed his Bowling Green studio, Cayce's partner withdrew from the business. Cayce stayed in Bowling Green to pay off his debts, while Gertrude returned to Hopkinsville with their son Hugh. Again family tragedy struck two years later when the Cayce's second son, Milton, developed whooping cough and colitis and died. Cayce blamed the child's death on his own lack of initiative for not starting readings on the boy.

During a Christmas visit to Hopkinsville, Cayce cured a local homeopath, Dr. Wesley Ketchum. Impressed by Cayce's abilities, Ketchum summoned Cayce's readings for many of his most difficult cases. He also spoke of Cayce's remarkable abilities to the audience of the American Association of Clinical Research in Boston. Moreover, Ketchum and a Hopkinsville hotel owner encouraged Cayce to join them in the establishment of the Psychic Reading Corporation, which would be Cayce's first formal psychic business venture. Similar to his earlier business partnership, this venture also failed. Cayce terminated the partnership in 1911 because of a dispute with Ketchum over the homeopath's acceptance of a fee for a reading.

Between 1911 and 1923, Cayce alternated between conducting readings and working as a photographer. During a reading, Cayce induced his own trance and then answered questions about a patient's medical condition. He never conducted research about the patient prior to his diagnosis. Moreover, his patients were not always physically present. His readings were full of biblical phrases and metaphors that reflected the spirituality of the Disciples of Christ Church. Initially Cayce teamed with some doctors in treating patients, but later found few doctors who would carry out his recommended treatments. As a result Cayce turned his attention toward opening a hospital attended by doctors, nurses, and staff who would carry out his treatment.

In 1923 theosophist Arthur Lammers brought Cayce to Dayton, Ohio, to give metaphysical readings. Although Cayce's treatments had been limited to health disorders, this meeting transitioned him toward conducting private readings for life disorders. Aligning with the theosophy tenets of karma and reincarnation, Cayce began giving readings that explored an individual's past or future lives. If he wanted to change the course of his own life, Cayce figured the time was now. After a brief stint in Dayton, Cayce sold his photography business and concentrated his efforts on building the foundation for his hospital. For the first time he started accepting donations for his readings.

Simple gratuity alone, however, could not fund Cayce's hospital plans. But a reading conducted on the pregnant wife of New York City businessman Morton Blumenthal proved to be fortuitous. Blumenthal, who valued Cayce's dream interpretations, financed the Edgar Cayce Hospital in Virginia Beach, Virginia. The location was revealed in a Cayce reading. By November 1928, patients from around the world were coming to the hospital for readings and treatment. The hospital, under the initial direction of Gertrude's brother-in-law T. B. House, a trained medical doctor and osteopath, did not have any formally trained medical doctors on staff. Most likely the lack of doctors was not by choice. Osteopathy, including naturopathy and chiropractic medicine, was considered fringe medicine during the early twentieth century

Cayce believed he often treated diseases from a patient's previous life, and treatments at Cayce Hospital ranged from hydrotherapy and colonic irrigation to radioactive and electrical treatment. Some of Cayce's treatments would seem outlandish by today's standards. For example, he often used turpentine and kerosene in treatment, recommended Jerusalem artichokes as a natural source of insulin, and advocated smoking in moderation. He believed certain animal blood serum and cyanic laetrile were cancer cures, and he theorized low levels of electrotherapy could help multiple sclerosis patients regain balance and facilitate the body's natural healing. Cayce emphasized preventive medicine and the relationship of the mind, body, and spirit in healing. Not all of his treatment measures were far-fetched, however. He noted man-made toxins could turn cancerous by overloading the system with "used tissue" that has the tendency to accumulate around bruises—which Cayce believed were likely sources of cancer.

In 1930, soon after the opening of the hospital, Cayce expanded his business philosophy by opening Atlantic University. But success was fleeting for the sleeping prophet. Within a span of two years, both the hospital and university were no longer operational. Blumenthal's fortune collapsed with the Great Depression, and Cayce was forced to start from scratch yet again.

Over the course of twenty-nine years, Cayce conducted over fourteen thousand psychic readings with more than nine hundred thousand documented transcribed texts. The founding of the Association for Research and Enlightenment (ARE) in June 1932 provided a safe house not only for Cayce's three thousand transcripts, but also for experimentation and education in holistic health care, extrasensory perception (ESP), meditation, spiritual healing, and life after death.

Edgar Cayce circa 1944

Later in life Cayce was besieged by so many requests for readings that his assistant had to schedule events two years in advance. Under the stress of popular demand, Cayce collapsed from exhaustion in 1944 and died the next year. After his death, associates bought back the Cayce Hospital in 1956 to continue psychic research. In the early 1980s several Cayce clinics throughout the United States operated treatment centers derived from Cayce's records. His heirs also formed the Edgar Cayce Foundation in 1992 and archived Cayce's 14,263 readings.

However, Cayce was not without critics who continued to ponder the scientific weight of his curing powers. Critics noted that the reading at the Bowling Green E.Q.B. Literary Club was the only instance in which his readings were conducted under a controlled setting, even though the setting was poorly controlled. No study with a controlled group was ever conducted to test Cayce's prescriptive treatment. Anecdotal evidence revealed that patients recovered, but nothing showed whether they had also been under the medical supervision of a trained doctor during the course of Cayce's prescribed treatment. Furthermore, Cayce's diagnostic abilities or cures were not tested on individuals who did not know him personally or had never heard of him.

Critics contend little, if any, follow-up with Cayce's patients can verify that his regimen offered legitimate healing. In Cayce's first public reading, for example, Aimee Dietrich had been attended by specialists. No mention was made, however, of the particular specialties. Also, it was only after Cayce's diagnosis that Aimee's mother recollected certain details. Cayce's reading noted that Aimee had struck the end of her spine while getting out of a carriage three years earlier, and the next day she came down with grippe. After hearing Cayce's statement, Mrs.

Dietrich claimed to remember the event, but insisted she had not mentioned the occurrence because her daughter appeared uninjured immediately after the accident. Moreover, no medical doctor ever followed up after Cayce's prescriptive treatment for the young girl.

Even if follow-up had been conducted, the medical background of those who claimed to be "doctors" during the late nineteenth and early twentieth centuries was suspect. Medical training at that time often consisted of infusions of homeopathy as part of the medical curriculum. It wasn't until the mid-1940s that US medical schools began a rigorous overhaul of the curriculum. Depending on the disorder, such as multiple sclerosis, certain conditions have patterns of remission that can be deceptive to the full healing process. The lack of modern diagnostic technology, such as MRIs, also thwarted the true validity of Cayce's treatment.

An examination of statistical records kept by the Cayce heirs also raises questions. A 1971 article written by Hugh and Edgar Cayce Jr., noted their study of 150 randomly chosen Cayce cases. Original requests for treatment, Cayce's readings, and patient follow-up letters were examined. The study reported sixty-five positive and eleven negative outcomes. Seventy-four sent no report at all, so the writers omitted them from their analysis. Thus the writers declared sixty-five out of seventy-six successes, or an 86 percent success rate. However, researchers question the reasons for half of the patients failing to write back or show up for a reading. Did they have negative responses to Cayce? Or had they possibly died before being able to respond?

No matter the naysayers, the medical community eventually paid attention to Edgar Cayce. In a 1979 editorial in the prestigious *Journal of the American Medical Association,* the association recognized Edgar Cayce as the father of holistic medicine and noted he was a primary influence in the development of the modern holistic medicine movement in America.

CHAPTER 12

The Haunting Death of Octavia Hatcher

In the heart of Pikeville, Kentucky, a life-size, full-length statue of an elegantly dressed young woman towers over Pikeville Cemetery. Engraved with the name of Octavia Hatcher, the tombstone is an eternal remembrance of a woman who lived for only twenty-one years. But some local residents insist that the tragedy of Octavia's horrific death makes it impossible for her soul to rest in peace—and that her spirit has haunted her final resting place since her death in 1891.

Very little is known about Octavia's short life. The few established facts about Octavia have revealed that her father, Jacob Smith, was one of the founders of Pikeville, and that she married a prominent local businessman, James Hatcher, in Pike County in 1889. At the time of their marriage, Octavia was nineteen years old, eleven years younger than her new husband.

Historical records have documented much more about the life of James Hatcher. One of nine children of a successful merchant, James was born in Floyd County, Kentucky, in 1859. His father operated several stores, including one in Pikeville, and stocked the retail establishments with merchandise shipped by boat from Pittsburgh, Pennsylvania.

Young James obviously inherited his father's entrepreneurial abilities. After completing his education in Pikeville, he immediately went into business for himself. At age eighteen he began a lifetime of successfully owning and operating a number of enterprises, including several businesses related to shipping. At one point he owned a large warehouse on the Big Sandy River and handled most of the goods shipped by steamboat to Pikeville. He also owned a timber operation and floated hundreds of rafts of timber from the Big Sandy River in eastern Kentucky to the Ohio River.

In partnership with several other Pikeville businessmen, James built and operated a steamboat, the *Mountain Girl,* on the Big Sandy River. He also had the joy of taking the last steamboat ride from Ashland to Pikeville on the steamer the *Mary Stewart.*

James wisely invested his profits in property located in Pike and Floyd Counties. After purchasing thirty-seven hundred acres of land for coal mining, he established the James Hatcher Coal Company. He also owned an additional six thousand acres of land, making him the largest landholder in Pike County. He even entered the local political arena, serving as clerk of the Pike County Court for four years and railroad commissioner for the district. Moreover, he dabbled in the building trade. In 1886 he contracted to build the courthouse in Pikeville.

While becoming one of the wealthiest businessmen in Pike County, James also found time to court the beautiful teen, Octavia Smith. After their marriage in 1889, the young couple immediately focused on starting a family. Their son Jacob was born in January 1891. But the joy of holding their firstborn son in their arms was short lived. Sadly, Jacob died only a few days after birth.

The cause of little Jacob's death is not known, although infant deaths from undisclosed illnesses were not uncommon in the nineteenth century. Since few, if any, medical facilities or physicians were available for delivering babies in the 1800s, infants were typically born at home with the assistance of a midwife or a helpful group of women from church or the neighborhood. Additionally, vaccines and medications for treating even common conditions had not yet been discovered. Babies, toddlers, and children under age ten suffered from a much higher mortality rate than the children of the twenty-first century.

The Hatchers were devastated by Jacob's death. Octavia, who had not fully recovered from childbirth, was so consumed by grief and depression that she rarely left her bed. Days soon turned into weeks, and Octavia's health and mental state failed to improve. After several months she slipped into a coma. Her breathing grew shallow, and all efforts to awaken her were unsuccessful. On May 2, 1891, Octavia Smith Hatcher was pronounced dead from unknown causes, less than four months after the death of her beloved son.

Since embalming was not a common practice at the time and the spring of 1891 was usually warm, a swift burial was planned for Octavia. Funeral services were held soon after her death, and her body was laid to rest in Pikeville Cemetery. A modest marker was placed at the site of her grave.

Death marks the end of life for most individuals, leaving their families with nothing more than fond memories. For Octavia Hatcher, however, death marked the beginning of a horrific tale, evolving into a legend that has continued to haunt the community.

A few days after Octavia's burial, several Pikeville residents began to experience symptoms similar to the mysterious condition that had ended Octavia's life. Frightened family members watched helplessly as their loved ones slipped into a deep coma and could not be aroused. The townspeople of Pikeville quickly labeled the illness as the "sleeping sickness."

Unlike Octavia, however, people in the community who had lapsed into a coma began to arouse from their deep sleep after only a few days. As James Hatcher learned of the rapid recovery of his friends and neighbors, a terrifying thought crossed his mind. Had he buried his wife too hastily? Could she, too, have emerged from her coma? Worse yet, had she been buried alive?

The grieving widower hastily arranged for an emergency exhumation of his wife's remains. As the casket was exhumed and the coffin lid opened, James and the group standing beside him were horrified by the sight. Octavia's sightless eyes were open wide, and a terrified expression was frozen on her face. The shredded lining on the lid of the coffin, along with Octavia's bloody fingers and broken nails, made it painfully clear that she had awakened from her coma in her grave. Octavia had been buried alive, trapped underground in her own coffin.

How could this have happened? Apparently, in the depths of her coma, Octavia had been so lifeless, her breath so shallow and faint, that the local physician had mistakenly believed she was no longer alive. Still, no one could identify the mysterious illness that had attacked Octavia and other members of community.

At the time, many people suspected the deadly tsetse fly had been the source of the mysterious illness. The tsetse fly feeds on the blood of animals and humans. Its bite carries a parasite that can work its way through the human body. High fevers, headaches, and joint aches are typical symptoms in the beginning stages. Once the parasite reaches the central nervous system, it often attacks the body's major organs. Pregnant women often suffer miscarriages. Victims become too weak to eat, drink, or function and eventually lapse into a deep sleep–like state and coma. The condition is commonly known as the "sleeping sickness," and death is the typical end result.

But the theory of the tsetse fly as the culprit of the condition that plagued Pikeville has never been proven. According to historical records, Africans fought against the sleeping sickness as early as the fourteenth century. An outbreak of sleeping sickness in Uganda killed four million people in 1906. Yet no records of sleeping sickness caused by the tsetse fly have ever been documented in the United States.

Eliminating the tsetse fly as a possible source for the mysterious Pikeville outbreak, what could have been the source? Some contend that yellow fever may have been the basis for the disease. Yellow fever, much like the sleeping sickness of the tsetse fly, is caused by an insect bite. Certain mosquitoes that thrive and breed in water spread the virus by biting humans. Initially the disease causes fevers, headaches, muscle aches, and loss of appetite. Progression of the disease often results in coma or death. In fact yellow fever results in death for almost half of those who develop severe symptoms. Survivors usually recover gradually over a period of several weeks.

Numerous yellow fever epidemics swept through the United States throughout the eighteenth and nineteenth centuries. When ships from the Caribbean docked at American ports, the vessels not only imported cargo, but also yellow fever. At first, the disease ran rampant through cities as far north as Boston. After 1822, however, most cases were reported in southern port cities and locations along the Mississippi River system.

A third, and the most common, theory comes from the coal industry that encompassed Pike County. Many people believed that toxic methane coal dust or the air emitted from the coal mines may have been a major factor in causing the puzzling illness. A finely powdered form of coal, coal dust is created by crushing or grinding coal. Since the texture of coal is brittle, mining or transporting coal can create tiny bits of coal dust that can be lifted into the air and spread over surrounding communities. To make matters worse, coal dust contains compounds of sulfur that can cause corrosion, and other toxic materials that are highly explosive.

Methane gases from the coal mines surrounding Pikeville may have had an impact on area residents, as well. Colorless and odorless, methane does not create physical reactions such as coughing or watery eyes. The gas will, however, cause suffocation if methane builds up in a space without proper ventilation.

Did a combination of deadly gases and toxic coal dust result in the horrific fate of Octavia Hatcher and the comas of other area residents? Or was a mystery virus caused by an insect bite the reason for the baffling disease?

Unfortunately, an accurate answer to the puzzling source of Octavia's death may never be found. Moreover, pinpointing the cause of her demise at the time of her death was next to impossible for James Hatcher and the community. Grief stricken and devastated, Octavia's husband never fully recovered from his wife's tragic death.

To honor Octavia's memory, James reburied his wife and replaced the simple grave marker with a full-length stone statue bearing a remarkable resemblance to Octavia. Erected directly

Octavia Hatcher statue in Pikeville Cemetery

over her grave, the monument featured the form of a beautiful young woman cradling a baby in her arms. The baby, of course, represented the Hatchers' son Jacob.

After Octavia's death, James plunged back into his work, continuing to build his business empire. But he never forgot his beautiful young bride. In later years he built a large hotel in Pikeville, erecting the structure so he could view his wife's cemetery monument from the hotel windows.

In 1916 James built another hotel in Pikeville, known as the Hotel James Hatcher, on the site now occupied by the East Kentucky Exposition Center. With two hundred rooms, the six-story hotel was constructed with steel. James advertised the hotel as "fireproof," assuring guests they could "sleep in safety."

James left his mark on the hotel, displaying his favorite quotations and sayings in writing on the lobby walls. He also opened a small museum in the reception area, displaying odd items, including an iron lung as an example of one of the newest pieces of medical equipment for saving lives.

Another, even stranger item on exhibit in the hotel lobby was a casket. Shortly before James died in 1939, he commissioned the building of his own customized casket. Knowing what his wife had experienced in her underground tomb, James was determined to make certain he could escape if he met the same fate. To quell his drastic phobia of being buried alive, James had the casket designed to latch on the inside and sealed with a special tool that could be removed only after burial.

Though James continued to make a name for himself long after Octavia's death, his wife has become the most famous Hatcher over the years. Attracted by the grisly story of her live burial, strangers began flocking to her grave to personally view the site. And a never-ending series of ghost tales have generated around Octavia's remains.

Pikeville residents living near the cemetery have reported hearing the cries of a kitten near Octavia's grave. But as they approached the plot to investigate the noise, the sounds mysteriously ended. Others have contended they could hear a woman crying in the same area of the cemetery.

One person claimed to have seen a vision of a person dressed in white near Octavia's grave. The vision screamed, "Oh, God, my baby is dead!" Other witnesses have sworn that they have encountered a wispy form floating among the graves in the cemetery. In recent years a photographer snapped an image of Octavia's statue on a clear, cloudless day. When the photographer looked at the print of the photo, she was astonished to discover a mysterious haze around Octavia's statue. Some believers have insisted that the photo is proof that Octavia's spirit remains in the cemetery.

At some point in time, vandals invaded the Pikeville Cemetery and maliciously broke the arm of Octavia's statue—the same arm that held the stone form of the Hatcher's infant son. Now the statue of the infant rests on his own grave, near the foot of his mother. The small stone marking the plot is inscribed with the words "Our Baby Jacob."

Since Pikeville Cemetery is located near Pike University in downtown Pikeville, the cemetery has been a favorite gathering spot for college students to party and investigate the ghost of Octavia Hatcher. Over the years students have reportedly heard screams coming from the direction of Octavia's grave.

According to a popular urban legend, Octavia's spirit becomes active each year on the anniversary of her death. As the story goes, her spirit spins her statue around to face the opposite direction, allowing her to "turn her back" on the town that had permitted her to be buried alive. Many years passed before residents of the community discovered that mischievous college students had always been the cause of the statue's odd behavior.

In the 1990s the Hatcher family erected a fence around the plot, attempting to thwart any future vandalism. They also erected a new marble base beneath the statue, not only to make the statue less accessible to vandals, but also to relate factual information about Octavia's life and death. Today visitors can read about Octavia on the inscribed portion of the marble base.

Sadly, Octavia Hatcher may not have been remembered at all if she had not experienced such a horrendous death in her own grave. But some believers insist that the young woman's spirit will never allow anyone to forget her last, torturous moments on Earth.

CHAPTER 13

The Spirits of Waverly Hills Sanatorium

In the early part of the twentieth century, a severe outbreak of tuberculosis swept through Jefferson County, Kentucky. To curtail the deadly disease, the local government opened a sanatorium in the southwestern portion of the county. More than a century later, the Waverly Hills Sanatorium now stands abandoned and forlorn. But everyone, from paranormal investigators to the current owners, insist that the spirits of those who died within its walls are haunting the place where they took their last breaths. Folklore, legends, and documented ghost investigations continue to perpetuate the mystique of Waverly Hills Sanatorium.

Today the sanatorium remains standing on property once owned by Major Thomas H. Hays. After purchasing the land in 1883, Hays built a home for his family on the property. A lack of nearby schools prompted him to open a one-room schoolhouse close to his home and hire a teacher to provide a quality education for his daughters.

The teacher's fondness for the Waverley novels written by Scottish novelist Sir Walter Scott inspired the name of Waverley for the school. Since the name also appealed to Hays, he named his property Waverley Hills.

With one of the highest tuberculosis rates in the country at the turn of the twentieth century, Jefferson County desperately needed a facility to house tuberculosis patients. Without a cure for the disease, the general course of treatment was to isolate patients from the public in hopes of curtailing the spread of tuberculosis. The medical philosophy was that victims of the "White Plague," as tuberculosis was often called, could benefit from fresh country air.

By 1908, officials with the city of Louisville and Jefferson County had authorized the purchase of a site to erect future buildings to care specifically for tuberculosis patients. After considering several sites, the Board of Tuberculosis Hospital purchased the Waverley Hills property and decided to keep the name of Waverley, at some point dropping the second *e* to become Waverly Hills.

A two-story, wooden structure was constructed on the property, containing administrative offices and two open-air pavilions. When the Waverly Hills Sanatorium opened on July 26, 1910, the facility offered a capacity of forty beds for treating patients in the early stages of tuberculosis. Edgewood, the

Waverly Hills Sanatorium

original home of the Hays family, became a nurses' dormitory and later was used as staff housing. It was eventually destroyed by fire.

In early 1911, as the city of Louisville prepared to build a new City Hospital, commissioners decided that tuberculosis patients should be treated in a separate facility and allocated twenty-five thousand dollars to construct a hospital to treat advanced cases of pulmonary tuberculosis. On August 31, 1912, all tuberculosis patients from City Hospital were relocated to temporary quarters in tents on the grounds of Waverly Hills, pending the completion of a hospital for advanced cases. In December 1912, a hospital for advanced cases opened for the treatment of another fifty patients. Later, with the opening of the main facility, this building became the Colored Hospital and later still was used as staff housing.

In 1916 a children's pavilion opened at Waverly Hills. One end of the building contained a furnished schoolroom for up to forty children. Young patients had access to a children's library, a motion picture machine, and playground equipment. During the holiday season, Santa visited the youngsters, his sleigh pulled by reindeer across the grounds of Waverly Hall. According to one source, the facility cared not only for sick children, but also for the children of tuberculosis patients who could not be properly cared for otherwise.

But the number of individuals needing treatment for tuberculosis rapidly outpaced the capacity of Waverly Hills. To accommodate the growing number of cases, construction began in 1924 on a five-story brick building that could house more than four hundred patients. After more than two years of construction, the new building opened on October 17, 1926.

A tunnel was also constructed to provide easier access to the new hospital, which was situated on a high, steep hill. The tunnel, measuring five hundred feet in length, ran from the base of the hill to the first floor of the building. Steps on one side of the tunnel provided a passageway for workers to enter and leave the hospital without trekking up or down the steep slope. On the other side of the tunnel, a motorized cable system with rails and carts allowed supplies to be transported to the top. A heating system, pipes, and air ducts also ran through the tunnel.

Since the sanatorium opened before the discovery of antibiotics to treat tuberculosis, heat lamps, fresh air, and positive attitudes were the standard methods of treatment. The staff made sure patients received plenty of sunshine and fresh air by rolling beds out to the solarium each day. Even during the chilly winter months, patients were always present on the solarium, tucked in their beds and covered with electric blankets so they could continue to be exposed to fresh air and sunlight throughout the year.

The staff worked hard to keep patients in high spirits, as well. To provide diversions from their illness, patients could participate in craft classes, watch movies, and listen to the radio through headphones. Horseback riding was even available for healthier patients.

Still, a cure for tuberculosis had yet to be discovered in the 1930s, and the death toll at Waverly Hills Sanatorium began to climb. At the height of the epidemic in 1945, records show that 162 deaths occurred at the sanatorium during the year. Although urban legends claim that hundreds of thousands of patients died at Waverly Hills, researchers contend that about eight thousand deaths from tuberculosis took place at the sanatorium over a period of fifty years.

The increasing number of deaths at Waverly Hills during the mid-1940s prompted hospital officials to find a method of discreetly removing the bodies from the facility, out of view from patients who might become distraught at the sight. The solution was to transport the bodies from the building through the tunnel. At the bottom of the hill, the corpses were placed into waiting hearses and quietly whisked away to mortuaries.

With the introduction of streptomycin as a treatment for tuberculosis during the 1940s, the number of tuberculosis cases gradually decreased. By the early 1960s, large hospitals designed specifically for treating tuberculosis patients were no longer necessary, and Waverly Hills Sanatorium closed its doors in 1961. Two years later the facility became a nursing home known as Woodhaven Geriatrics Center, primarily treating aging patients with mental and physical limitations. Woodhaven operated at the site for nearly twenty years, until the state closed the center for inappropriate patient care.

Abandoned of occupants and lacking usefulness around 1980, the vacant building soon fell into disrepair. Boarded and broken windows, trash around the grounds, and graffiti on the walls gave way to a spooky atmosphere that became a destination for the homeless and a hangout for wayward teens. With the morbid history of Waverly Hills Sanatorium, rumors and legends began to circulate about the building's past occupants and the possibilities that the decrepit facility was the center of a high volume of paranormal activity.

One of the first myths about Waverly Hills Sanatorium concerned the use of the tunnel. Legends surfaced that the tunnel had actually served as a body chute or death tunnel for sliding dead bodies from the facility to the bottom of the hill. Though corpses were moved from the sanatorium through the tunnel, records indicate the tunnel had never been used as a slide to roll bodies down the hill.

Still, with the passage of time, the legends and myths continued to escalate as the abandoned building took on an even more haunting atmosphere. One of the most prominent legends revolves around a nurse who worked at Waverly Hills. Depressed from caring for so many suffering patients, she hanged herself in Room 502. Another local version of the legend claims the unmarried nurse had discovered she was pregnant by the owner of the sanatorium. To make matters worse, she had also contracted tuberculosis. Distraught, she hanged herself with a light bulb wire.

Paranormal investigators have reported evidence of a higher amount of paranormal activity in Room 502 than in any other room in Waverly Hills Sanatorium. The investigators claim that since ghosts are a form of energy, they disrupt natural electromagnetic fields in their vicinity; therefore, electromagnetic field (EMF) meters can be used to detect those disruptions. Though variations in EMF meter readings do not provide solid proof of the presence of a ghost, paranormal researchers insist the readings are strong indicators of a ghostly presence.

In Room 502, EMF meters have detected such forceful and lengthy disturbances that the equipment has actually stopped functioning. Cameras, too, have suddenly malfunctioned in the room, even though they resumed working perfectly when investigators moved to other areas of the building.

Another popular myth contends a young woman known as Mary often peers out of a third-floor window. Although no proof has ever been found of Mary's presence, a woman claiming to be a psychic offered some remarkable insights into the mystery during a visit to Waverly Hills in 2000. The individual who owned the building at the time, along with his security staff, found the psychic wandering through the corridor on the third floor. The psychic indicated she had been drawn to Waverly, particularly to the third floor, by a spirit named Mary. Since the legend of Mary was well-known, the owner was not totally convinced of the woman's claim of being a psychic. But just as he was getting ready to escort her from the premises, she entered one of the rooms. The woman paused, announced that this was the room once occupied by Mary, and instructed the owner to look in the closet. There, she insisted, he would discover some items that had belonged to Mary.

The owner peered into the closet, finding nothing until the woman directed him to reach behind a broken portion of plaster on the rear wall. To the owner's amazement, he pulled out a large serving fork. She insisted that if he tried again, he would find more items. Following her instructions, he reached behind the wall and pulled out a lady's slipper and three photographs. One photo was a simple shot of a road surrounded by woods. The second photo featured four men sitting on a brick wall. The last picture showcased a young woman who appeared to be in her early twenties. When the owner looked at the back of the photograph, he was astonished to see a handwritten name: Mary Lee. He looked up to see a satisfied smile on the psychic's face. Without saying another word, she turned and left the room. The owner never saw her again.

The spirit of a little boy also is rumored to linger at Waverly Hills Sanatorium. According to urban legend and paranormal investigators, the youngster runs through the building, playing with a small leather ball that was common in the 1920s and 1930s. The boy is known by several different names, including Timmy, Johnny, and Tommy.

During one all-night investigation that took place on Halloween in the early 2000s, a group of ghost hunters placed a fluorescent light in the hallway, along with a camera. Within a short time the group witnessed a humanlike shape about the size of a small boy cross the hallway. Ironically, the group did not realize the video camera had captured the image until they watched the footage. One member of the group claimed to have personally encountered the little boy. In another incident that occurred during a tour of the lower level of the building, a guide tripped over a small leather ball. After the tour group left the premises, the guide returned to the lower level and discovered the ball was missing. He later found the ball on the fifth floor of the building. Had the spirit of the little boy moved his toy to another location?

While everyone admits the interior portion of the building emits an eerie atmosphere, others have observed strange happenings on the grounds of Waverly Hills Sanatorium. On one recent occasion—decades after the last patient had died or been discharged from the facility—a lone security guard was standing watch in the parking lot one evening while his colleagues left the premises to get dinner. Suddenly he noticed a hearse enter through the open gates to the grounds, drive up to the building, and stop at the old loading dock. Two men wearing white hospital-style attire got out of the car and entered a door that led to an area that once had been used as the morgue.

Within moments the men emerged from the building, hauling a large, rectangular boxlike object. One of the men swung open the rear door of the hearse, and the interior lights automatically came on in the car. Even through dusk was rapidly approaching, the lights inside the car allowed the guard to clearly identify the object being loaded into the hearse: a casket. Horrified, the guard stood frozen in place as the men got back into the hearse and drove away.

By the time the other security guards returned to the grounds, the remaining guard was nowhere to be found. The next day, the head of security called the guard and asked why he had abandoned his post in the middle of his shift. After relating the mysterious incident to his boss, the guard declared that nothing could ever get him to return to Waverly.

In addition to inexplicable events and the presence of ghostly spirits, visitors to the abandoned hospital have also reported witnessing strange lights, shapes, and noises. Dozens of people have heard the sounds of doors slamming in distant parts

of the building, even during times when the wind was not blow-
ing and the air was perfectly still.

Shadowy shapes described by witnesses as dark humanlike
images move up and down the hallways and in and out of rooms
so frequently that one floor is known as the "Hall of Shadows."
Often more than one person witness the shadows.

In 2004 one ghost-hunting group tried to capture the
"shadow people" on film. The group set up a laser grid in the
rooms on the fourth floor. Motion detectors in the corners of
the rooms emitted laser beams. When they watched the film,
the group saw shadowy images move through the lasers. The
mass of the shadows broke the beams, and the motion detector
went off.

Many photographs taken inside the hospital have revealed
mysterious orbs. Since particles of dust are often floating through
the old, abandoned building, however, orbs cannot be presented
as reliable evidence of the paranormal.

Faint red lights have also been seen with no natural explanation for their existence. On one occasion a brilliant white light
leaped across a hallway, then disappeared as quickly as it had
materialized. Video cameras have captured balls of lights moving
down the halls at incredible speed, images that looked like the
shadow of person walking in one of the rooms. One investigator
using an infrared camera captured an image of a headless ghost
walking past her in the hallway. The image appeared to be a large
man wearing a white uniform.

Many people regard the fourth floor as the most frightening area of the hospital. The entrance to the area is usually locked. Portions of the floor have caved in, and some areas are not safe to enter. One of the primary reasons for the fourth floor's scary reputation is the bone-chilling experience of a paranormal investigator in a fourth-floor room that had once been used as a treatment area. Using an EMF meter, the investigator picked up intense readings in the room. Behind him, two members of his investigative group were filming the scene with a video camera. As he watched the meter, something suddenly hit him in the back. Just as he realized he had been struck by an empty soda bottle, one end of an overhead fluorescent light fixture broke loose, swinging down from the ceiling and knocking him in the head. The fluorescent tube in the fixture shattered into tiny pieces, showering him with shards of glass.

Before he could catch his breath, the investigator heard the sound of a brick being scraped across the concrete floor. In an instant, the brick flew directly at him. With no time to get out of the way, he turned just as the brick struck him in the small of the back.

The investigator and his friends fled the room. Not until much later did they check the videotape. Amazingly, the camera had captured the bottle and light fixture crashing into him and the brick moving across the floor. Since the camera was focused directly on the investigator, no one could figure out how the bottle had flown across the room.

A member of a tour group at Waverly Hills left the premises with another disturbing story. While touring the Hall of
Shadows, the man saw a shadow about four feet high pass in
front of him. Then the object silently moved across the room
and disappeared through the wall.

Back at the hotel, the man took off his shirt and noticed
several red welts and scratches on the left side of his torso. Peering into the mirror, he could see the marks spelled the word *Dad,*
along with an X and an O appearing to be underlined. He could
not remember coming into contact with anything that might
have made the marks on his skin. Moreover, the welts had not
caused any pain. But as soon as he touched the area, his skin felt
like it was burning. The next morning the marks had mysteriously vanished. Had the shadow person left a temporary mark on
him as they passed in the hall at Waverly Hills?

Since the last geriatric patient left the facility in 1982, various developers and owners have had grand plans for converting
Waverly Hills into various profitable business ventures. In 1983,
for instance, a developer bought the hospital for more than three
million dollars, intending to convert the site into a minimum-
security state prison. Plans failed, however, especially after
neighbors protested the idea. A religious foundation purchased
Waverly Hills and the grounds during the 1990s with plans to
construct a worship center on the site, along with the world's
tallest statue of Jesus. After raising only three thousand dollars
for the effort, the group canceled the project in December 1997.

In 2001 a married couple with family members who had been treated for tuberculosis at Waverly Hills purchased the sanatorium with the intent of restoring the building and preserving its historical value. Considering the vast interest in the old sanatorium, Charlie and Tina Mattingly decided to offer overnight ghost investigations, historical tours, and annual Halloween activities to help fund their restoration efforts. They also established a nonprofit historical association for Waverly Hills.

Along the way the bizarre events at Waverly Hills Sanatorium have attracted both national and international audiences. Television shows have labeled Waverly Hills as one of the most haunted hospitals in the United States. The facility has been featured on numerous television programs, including the Travel Channel's *Ghost Adventures,* the Sci-Fi Channel's *Ghost Hunters,* and the Family Channel's *Scariest Places on Earth.* Even French and British television programs have featured the sanatorium and its legends. Moreover, a horror film, *Death Tunnel,* and a documentary, *Spooked,* were filmed at Waverly Hills in 2004. Both movies were released in 2006.

Are spirits lingering in the old tuberculosis hospital and harboring secrets from the rest of us? Paranormal investigators are convinced that the site is one of the most haunted places on Earth—but the mysteries of the Waverly Hills Sanatorium continue to raise questions that have yet to be answered.

CHAPTER 14

The Mysteries of Mammoth Cave

Far beneath the surface of the hills in the southwestern part of Kentucky lies Mammoth Cave, the largest known cave in the world. The cave's dark crevices, endless passages, and echoing sounds have fascinated people for more than two centuries—and have created the perfect setting for mysteries, legends, and ghostly spirits to roam.

Experts say prehistoric man first set foot into Mammoth Cave some four thousand years ago. Perhaps believing the mysterious underground world offered passages to the afterlife, they used the site as a burial ground. Over the years multiple mummies have been discovered inside the depths of the cave, remarkably preserved by the underground environment. Native American artifacts have also been unearthed in Mammoth Cave, providing evidence that Indian tribes also explored the site.

Legends claim that the first white man entered the cave at the end of the eighteenth century as he chased a bear into the entrance. About the same time, the first legal owner claimed the site as part of a two-hundred-acre land grant. The property exchanged hands several times, until new owners purchased the cave in 1810 with the intent of mining saltpeter, a mineral used in the production of gunpowder.

Mining operations prospered at Mammoth Cave during the War of 1812. More than seventy slaves worked the operation, and many died during the grueling and miserable labor. When the war ended, however, so did the demand for saltpeter, and the mining operations at the cave were shut down. But word of the cave's contributions to the war effort—as well as the odd "mummies" found in the cave—had become well-known, and soon visitors starting arriving to see the immense underground caverns.

In 1838 an attorney from Glasgow, Kentucky, Franklin Gorin, realized the potential of Mammoth Cave as a tourist site, purchased the property, and immediately began to increase accessibility to the remote area by improving the roads that led to the cave. He also decided to use guides for leading groups of tourists through the maze of underground passages. Since few people knew about the intricate twists and turns of the cavern, he introduced a sixteen-year-old slave, Stephen Bishop, to the world of Mammoth Cave in the hopes that the young boy would become an expert cave guide.

Gorin was not disappointed in his choice of Bishop. The personable young slave became devoted to Mammoth Cave, exploring remote passages where no man had ever ventured.

Mammoth Cave National Park

Within a few months of arriving at the cave, Bishop placed a ladder over a deep hole in the cavern known as the "Bottomless Pit" and became the first person to cross over the pit to the other side. A bridge was soon constructed to span the pit so Bishop could share the wonders on the other side of the cave with visitors. Bishop was also the first to discover the cave's underground water system, more than twenty miles of passages, and blind albino fish swimming in the underground Echo River. Most important, he was the first man to explore and map the cave system.

Newspapers across the country spread the word about Bishop's discoveries, bringing even more visitors to the cave, and Gorin added two more slaves to work as tour guides. Although Bishop gained his freedom in 1856, he died the following year of unknown causes. The remaining guides continued leading cave tours until the 1870s, and their children carried on the family tradition for over a century. Several of the early guides, including Bishop, are buried at the Old Guide's Cemetery, located at Mammoth Cave National Park.

When Dr. John Croghan of Louisville purchased the cave for ten thousand dollars in 1839, the property included the slaves who were working as tour guides. Mammoth Cave prospered under Croghan's ownership. To provide accommodations for tourists near the site, he constructed a large inn, the Mammoth Cave Hotel, which served travelers until it burned down in 1916. Croghan also spent large sums of money on advertising that attracted visitors from all over the world.

A Louisville native who earned a doctorate in medicine from the University of Pennsylvania in 1813, Croghan had spent several years traveling abroad before returning to Louisville and opening a medical practice. After purchasing Mammoth Cave,

Croghan believed the cavern's moist atmosphere and constant temperature of fifty-four degrees might help cure tuberculosis patients. As a physician he was well aware of tuberculosis patients who had been cured of the deadly disease, known at the time as "consumption," by receiving treatment in European hospitals that were located underground.

Within three years of purchasing Mammoth Cave, Croghan directed his tour guides to construct eleven huts within the cave. Fifteen tuberculosis patients soon moved into the huts to be part of his experiment. Unfortunately, two patients died in the cave within the first year. The condition of the remaining patients worsened, and the "consumptive colony" was abandoned. Moreover, Croghan also contracted tuberculosis and died from the disease in 1849.

Today visitors can see reminders of the unsuccessful experiment at Mammoth Cave. Several tuberculosis patients who did not survive were buried in the Old Guide's Cemetery near the cave entrance, and the cave still holds the "consumptive cabins" that were constructed of wood and stone. A slab of stone, known as "Corpse Rock," sits in front of one of the cabins. Guides say it is the same stone that once held the bodies of dead tuberculosis patients before they were removed from the cave. And some visitors have reported hearing coughing in this part of the cave. Were they hearing echoes of the past?

Between prehistoric man and Native Americans who became trapped and eventually died in the cave, to accidents from the saltpeter operations and the deaths of tuberculosis victims, the odd reports from Mammoth Cave suggest that some former occupants may have never left the darkness of the underground world. Even park rangers, geologists, and scientists have encountered eerie sounds, physical touches, and ghostly apparitions that cannot be explained. In fact more than 150 paranormal events have been documented at Mammoth Cave, which has been called the "most haunted natural wonder in the world."

In recent years park rangers have reported strange incidents in an area of the cave where miners once held religious services, known as the "Methodist Church." At this point on a guided tour, a park ranger turns off the electric lights. During the blackout, tourists have the opportunity to experience the cave in much the same way that visitors viewed the underground world before the invention of batteries, flashlights, and electricity. Only the glow of an oil lantern shines over the area as the ranger speaks to the group.

During one recent tour, three guides led a large group into the Methodist Church. One of the guides stood at the back of the group as the lead guide turned off the electric lights. Without warning, the guide in the back felt a strong push on her shoulder. To keep from losing her balance, she took a step forward.

Assuming the third guide was standing next to her, she lowered her voice to a whisper and laughingly warned him to stop teasing her. In the next instant, the lead guide ignited a lantern, sending a warm glow over the area. To her astonishment, the guide realized her fellow guide was standing about seventy feet away. It would have been impossible for him to have shoved her and then walk through the darkness to the other side of the crowd.

At the end of another blackout in the Methodist Church, a guide weaved his way through the tour group, heading down the pathway to turn the electric lights back on. Through the glow of the lantern, he saw a black man wearing white pants, a white vest, a dark shirt, and a white hat with a floppy brim—attire similar to the clothing that the slaves who had once been tour guides might have worn. Standing next to him were his wife and two children.

The guide turned on the lights and spun back around to face the group. Amazingly he could not find a single African-American person in the crowd. The black man and his family had vanished. On other occasions visitors have reported seeing a similar sight and assumed that the black man in period dress had been part of a historical tour. But, like the ranger, visitors have contended that the man disappeared before they could ask him any questions.

On separate occasions visitors have asked one former cave guide about the man dressed in old-fashioned attire, standing some distance away near a pile of rocks. During both tours the man was seen at the same spot. And both times, the man vanished before anyone could approach him.

Was the image created by the eerie shadows in the cave? Was it a figment of overactive imaginations? Or was Stephen Bishop, the first cave guide, returning to the cave he loved?

While many have assumed the ghostly figure was Bishop, the former cave guide is not the only spirit that may still be haunting Mammoth Cave. A detailed article appearing in the February 1858 issue of *Knickerbocker* magazine, "A Tragedy in Mammoth Cave," related the tale of a young woman who lost the love of her life in the depths of the caverns.

Melissa, an impressionable young girl who lived near Mammoth Cave, decided to play a trick on her tutor, a Boston native named Beverleigh. Though she had fallen in love with the man, he had rejected her affections. To make matters worse, the tutor had started to court another girl in the area.

Somehow, Melissa convinced Beverleigh to accompany her to Mammoth Cave. Having grown up in the region, she was familiar with the winding, dark trails in the caverns. When they came to Echo River, an underground stream deep within the cave, she slipped into a side passage and left Beverleigh alone to find his own way back to the cave entrance.

Playing the cruel joke on the tutor out of spite and revenge, Melissa returned home. But days passed without any word from Beverleigh. Horrified by the possibilities that he may have never emerged from the cave, Melissa returned to the site to search for him. Day after day she resumed her underground quest, calling out his name until her voice became hoarse and raw. To her dismay Beverleigh was never seen again.

A few years later Melissa contracted tuberculosis. On her deathbed she confessed to the terrible trick that she had played on her tutor. Many family members and friends suspected she had been filled with guilt over his death. Even more people believe that her spirit is still seen and heard in Mammoth Cave as she continues to search for her lost love.

In recent years several tour guides took a boat ride on the Echo River and heard the voice of a woman calling out, as though she were looking for someone. At the time, they were unaware of Melissa's story. The next day an older guide related the tale of Melissa abandoning Beverleigh near the stream and revealed she had later died of tuberculosis. A few days later one of the guides took a new employee to see Echo River. Suddenly she grabbed his arm. "Did you hear a woman cough?" she asked. The guide felt a cold chill creep down his spine, remembering that Melissa had died of tuberculosis. The new employee also revealed she had heard voices wafting through the cave and had even heard someone whisper her name.

Melissa's spirit, however, may not be roaming alone through the cavern. Another tragic story occurred in the depths of the cave system during the twentieth century, and the incident created yet another haunting legend.

In 1917 explorer Floyd Collins discovered nearby Crystal Cave. A native of the area, Collins long suspected that Crystal Cave was somehow connected to Mammoth Cave—and he was determined to find a passage that would link the two caves together.

Collins knew about a narrow, twisting underground hole that was often called "Sand Cave" and talked about exploring the crevice. But his parents opposed his idea. His father warned him that the hole was far too dangerous and narrow to explore. And his mother confessed that she had a disturbing dream about her son getting hurt in a rock fall in the cave. The dream had been so vivid and real that she had seen angels coming to his aid, and she was convinced that the dream had been a warning from God.

Collins refused to listen to his parents' objections. On Friday morning, January 30, 1925, he entered Sand Cave and wedged his way through the tight passageways. At one point he inched his way on his stomach. When his lantern began to dim, he decided not to venture any farther, fearing he did not have enough lantern oil to continue his exploration for an extended period of time.

As he headed back to the cave entrance, a twenty-seven-pound boulder broke loose along the passageway and crushed his left foot. Pinned against the stone wall and lying on his right side, Collins was trapped. The light of his lantern soon went out, leaving him alone in the dark.

When Collins failed to return home the next day, his family and friends immediately launched a search-and-rescue effort. Soon engineers and geologists were summoned to the scene, as well as the Louisville Fire Department and experienced cavers. Some rescuers managed to reach Collins, providing him with necessary supplies for his survival. The dangerous, narrow passageway, however, prevented most rescuers from venturing too far into the crevice.

By Monday morning, reporters from across the country had congregated outside Sand Cave and started filing hourly updates on the tragedy. Several aviators, including the famous Charles Lindbergh, delivered news reports by air. A few reporters attempted to reach Collins for interviews, including William Burke Miller, a rookie reporter from the *Louisville Courier-Journal.*

With his small physique, Miller had been labeled "Skeets" by his colleagues for being as small as a mosquito. But Skeets Miller used his diminutive frame to his advantage, sliding down into the crevice, sitting with Collins and conducting interviews with the trapped explorer. Miller quickly relayed his reports to readers, who were enthralled with the firsthand accounts of the man who had been buried alive. Miller eventually won the Pulitzer Prize for his coverage of the tragedy.

Days turned into weeks as rescuers attempted various methods to extract Collins from the cave. Fascinated by daily on-the-scene reports, thousands of people traveled across the country and descended upon the area. A carnival atmosphere quickly evolved at the site, with hawkers selling food, drink, and souvenirs. At one point the Commonwealth of Kentucky dispatched military troops to uphold law and order.

The plight of Floyd Collins soon expanded into a national rescue effort, attracting the National Guard and the Red Cross to the scene. Collins's father offered a reward to anyone who could rescue his son. A group of rescuers finally widened the passage and tried to pry the rock from Collins's crushed foot. In the process, however, small cave-ins sent rescuers scurrying back to the surface. Fearing the shaft might collapse, the workers refused to return to the cave. One of Collins's friends, Johnny Gerald, was the last person to speak with him before the last cave-in.

Since reaching Collins through the crevice was no longer an option, miners started digging a vertical shaft to reach him. Working zealously, the volunteers finally reached Collins eighteen days after his initial entrapment. But their efforts were in vain. Collins had died three days before the shaft was completed. Ironically, he died on the unlucky February day of Friday the thirteenth.

Two months passed before rescuers could finally remove Collins's corpse from the cave. Originally family members conducted a burial service for Collins inside the cave, but his brother later had the body exhumed and reburied at the family's farm. In 1927 Collins's father sold the farm, which included Crystal Cave. Though family members protested the father's deal with the new owner, the sale did not include any mention of the removal of Collins's remains.

Envisioning a moneymaking attraction, the new owner exhumed Collins's body from the family farm. To everyone's surprise, however, he did not rebury the body. Instead he placed the corpse in a bronzed metal coffin, topped by a glass seal, and placed it on display at Crystal Cave in 1927 for tourists to view. The owner also placed a large granite tombstone at the head of the coffin.

Still, poor Collins could not rest in peace. In 1929 his corpse was stolen from the glass coffin. Authorities and bloodhounds from three counties were summoned to help with the search. The body was soon recovered near the cave, wrapped in burlap bags and hidden in the brush. But the rescuers were horrified to discover that the left leg was missing from Collins's corpse.

After the attempted theft, Collins's body was returned to the cave, and workers were instructed to cover and lock the casket each night with a metal lid. The body was occasionally displayed in the cave until 1951. He was later reburied—once again—inside Crystal Cave. In 1989 he was moved to his final resting place in Flint Ridge Cemetery, a few miles from the entrance to Mammoth Cave. Unfortunately Collins's missing leg was never recovered, and the thieves were never found.

Floyd Collins has not been forgotten. In fact his theory that Crystal Cave and other caves in the area were extensions of the larger Mammoth Cave system was eventually proven correct. And as people learned about the interconnecting passages, many wanted to convert the system of underground pathways into a national park to protect the site for future generations. By July 1941 President Franklin D. Roosevelt had authorized the Mammoth Cave system to receive National Park status.

The area that once trapped Floyd Collins has not been open to the public in recent years, although Crystal Cave has been mapped and charted by National Park Service employees.

And several of those employees have been convinced that Collins's spirit remains alive and well within the cave that buried him alive.

On one occasion several employees noticed an old whiskey bottle resting on a ledge in Crystal Cave as they headed into the cavern. When two of the men walked back to the cave entrance and passed by the bottle, they heard a strange noise. One employee later explained that the noise sounded as though someone had tapped a finger against the glass bottle, right behind his ear. Just as he turned around, he saw the bottle hit the ground.

The second employee, who had seen the incident, claimed the bottle had not just fallen, but had come straight out of the stone wall and dropped to the ground in front of him. Neither man had any explanation for the bizarre sight. Had the ghost of Floyd Collins been responsible for hurling a whiskey bottle at the men?

On another occasion in June 1976, two cave employees spent the day conducting a study on groundwater flow near the crevice that had entrapped Collins more than a half-century earlier. While one of the men went to check the level of a nearby spring, the other waited near the truck. Within a few minutes he heard the faint sound of a man calling out for help. "Help me! Help me!" the voice called out repeatedly. "I'm trapped! Johnny, help me!"

The man felt a cold chill run down his spine. He was vividly aware that Collins had been trapped in the nearby cave. As soon as his partner returned from the spring, the man related what he had heard. Not wanting to wait around to hear anything else, the two men hastily drove off.

Could the voice have belonged to Floyd Collins? Could the call for "Johnny" have referred to Johnny Gerald, the last person to speak with Collins? Is his spirit still trapped in the cave, or could the sound have been merely an eerie echo from long ago?

Today both employees and visitors still report unexplainable happenings at Mammoth Cave. Lanterns go off and on without warning, apparitions vanish as suddenly as they appear, and unexplained voices echo through the depths of the cave. Are the stories of Mammoth Cave merely figments of overactive imaginations? Or are ghosts truly present? Though the mysteries may never be solved, the tragedies and legends of Mammoth Cave have made it one of the most fascinating places in the world.

BIBLIOGRAPHY

CHAPTER 1: THE MYSTERY OF THE WELSH INDIANS

Avery, Roberta. "Will DNA turn Madoc myth into reality?"
Toronto Star (Canada). 2007. Newspaper Source,
*EBSCO*host database. Accessed September 11, 2011.

Herman, Linda. "The Legend of Prince Madoc." *Cricket.*
2008, 35(10): p. 4. Masterfile Premier, *EBSCO*host database.
Accessed September 11, 2011.

Kramer, Carl E. *Visionaries, Adventurers, and Builders:
Historical Highlights of the Falls of the Ohio.* Jeffersonville, IN:
Sunnyside Press, 1999.

Olson, Dana. *The Legend of Prince Madoc and the White
Indians.* Jeffersonville, IN: Olson Enterprises, 1987.

Traxel, William L. *Footprints of the Welsh Indians.* New York:
Algora Publishing, 2004.

CHAPTER 2: THE SEARCH FOR JONATHAN SWIFT'S SILVER MINES

Anonymous. "Search Continues for Swift's Lost Mine and
Buried Treasure." *The Kentucky Explorer.* 1906, 9(40):
53–57.

Dougherty, James. "The Legend of Swift's Silver Mine," 2003, http://web.archive.org/web/20070821113109/ and www.rootsweb.com/~vawise/SilverMine/LegendJAD. html. Accessed February 28, 2012.

Hamilton, Emory. "Swift's Silver Mine," August 1940. http://web.archive.org/web/20070820144919/ and www.rootsweb.com/~vawise/SilverMine/SSminesEH.html. Accessed February 28, 2012.

Jameson, W. C. *Buried Treasures of the Appalachians: Legends of Homestead Caches, Indian Mines, and Loot from the Civil War Raids.* Little Rock, AR: August House, Inc., 1991.

Nickell, Joe. *Ambrose Bierce Is Missing and Other Historical Mysteries.* Lexington: University Press of Kentucky, 2005.

Perrin, W. H. "Old Account Tells of Famed Silver Mine of John Swift." *The Kentucky Explorer.* 1885, 13(6): pp. 18–19.

Steely, Michael S. *Swift's Silver Mines and Related Appalachian Treasures.* Johnson City, TN: The Over Mountain Press, 1995.

CHAPTER 3: WHO REALLY INVENTED BOURBON WHISKEY?

Augustyn, Frederick. "Heaven Hill Distilleries and Bourbon Tasting Tour: Kentucky Culture and History in Bardstown's Heaven Hill Distilleries Bourbon Heritage Center." *The Public Historian.* Fall 2008, 30(4): pp. 110–115.

Carson, Gerald. *The Social History of Bourbon.* Lexington: The University Press of Kentucky, 1963.

Luntz, Perry. *Whiskey & Spirits for Dummies.* Hoboken, NJ: Wiley Publishing, Inc., 2008.

McDaniel, Susan. "Bourbon's Keeper: Bourbon Historian Mike Veach Keeps the Spirit's Fire Burning-Literally." *Imbibe: Liquid Culture.* May/June 2009. imbibemagazine.com/Bourbon-s-Keeper-Mike-Veach. Accessed May 7, 2012.

Waymack, Mark. *The Book of Classic American Whiskeys.* Peru, IL: Open Court Publishing Company, 1995.

CHAPTER 4: SECRETS OF THE OLD TALBOTT TAVERN

Brown, Alan. *Stories from the Haunted South.* Jackson: University Press of Mississippi, 2004.

Holland, Jeffrey Scott. *Weird Kentucky.* New York: Sterling Publishing Co., Inc., 2008.

Kleber, John E., Ed. *The Kentucky Encyclopedia.* Lexington: University Press of Kentucky, 1992.

Montell, William Lynwood. *Haunted Houses and Family Ghosts of Kentucky.* Lexington: University Press of Kentucky, 2001.

Nickell, Patti. "Bardstown is brimming with history." kentucky.com/2012/04/01/2134858/bardstown-is-brimming-with-history.html. Accessed March 3, 2013.

"Our place in Bourbon history." talbotts.com/index.php/our-place-in-bourbon-history/. Accessed February 19, 2013.

Starr, Patti Accord. *Ghosthunting Kentucky.* Cincinnati: Clerisy Press, 2010.

CHAPTER 5: WHAT CAUSED LIVESTOCK TO TREMBLE?

Bidwell, Chris. "White Snakeroot—*Ageratina Altissima* (L.) R. M. King and H. E. Robins." *Kentucky Naturalist News*. Spring 2009, 67(1): 7–9. www.ksnh.org/newsletters/KSNH-KNN-2009-1-1.pdf. Accessed September 29, 2011.

Christensen, William. "Milk Sickness: A Review of the Literature." *Economic Botany*. 1965, 19(3): 293–300. www.jstor.org/stable/4252612. Accessed October 1, 2011.

Daly, Walter. "The 'Slows': The Torment of Milk Sickness on the Midwest Frontier." *Indiana Magazine of History*. 2006, 102(1): 29–40. www.jstor.org/stable/27792690. Accessed October 1, 2011.

Jordan, Edwin and Norman Harris. "Milksickness." *The Journal of Infectious Diseases*. 1909, 6(4): 401–491. www.jstor.org/stable/30071608. Accessed October 1, 2011.

"Milk-Sickness." *The British Medical Journal*. 1883, 2(1187): 636–637. www.jstor.org/stable/25264218. Accessed September 27, 2011.

Niederhofer, Relda. "The Milk Sickness: Drake on Medical Interpretation." *The Journal of the American Medical Association*. 1985, 254(15): 2123–2125.

CHAPTER 6: MIKE FINK: THE LEGENDARY "MISSISSIPPI RIVER ALLIGATOR HORSE"

Allen, Michael. "Sired by a Hurricane: Mike Fink, Western Boatmen and the Myth of the Alligator Horse." *Arizona and the West*. 1985, 27(3): 237–252.

Allen, Michael. *Western Rivermen, 1763-1861: Ohio and Mississippi Boatmen and the Myth of the Alligator Horse.* Baton Rouge: Louisiana State University Press, 1994.

Blair, Walter and F. J. Meine (eds.). *Half Horse Half Alligator: The Growth of the Mike Fink Legend.* Chicago: University of Chicago Press, 1956.

Casseday, Ben. *The History of Louisville, from its Earliest Settlement till the Year 1852.* Louisville: Hull and Brother, 1852.

Field, Joseph. "Mike Fink," in Walter Blair and F. J. Meine (eds.) *Half Horse Half Alligator: The Growth of the Mike Fink Legend.* Chicago: University of Chicago Press, 1847.

Leeming, David and Jake Page. *Myths, Legends, and Folktales of America: An Anthology.* New York: Oxford University Press, 1999.

Smith, Thomas Rhys. *River of Dreams: Imaging the Mississippi before Mark Twain.* Baton Rouge: Louisiana State University Press, 2007.

CHAPTER 7: THE GHOSTS OF LIBERTY HALL

Brown, Alan. *Haunted Places in the American South.* Jackson: University Press of Mississippi, 2002.

"Liberty Hall Historic Site." libertyhall.org/johnbrown.htm. Accessed February 17, 2013.

McCormick, James and Macy Wyatt. *Ghosts of the Bluegrass.* Lexington: The University Press of Kentucky, 2009.

Montell, William Lynwood. *Tales of Kentucky Ghosts.* Lexington: The University Press of Kentucky, 2010.

Norman, Michael and Beth Scott. *Historic Haunted America.* New York: Tor Books, 1995.

CHAPTER 8: THE GHOSTLY SPIRITS OF WHITE HALL

"Cassius M. Clay." White Hall Clermont Foundation. whitehall clermontfoundation.org/html/cassius_clay.html. Accessed May 15, 2013.

McQueen, Keven. *Cassius M. Clay: Freedom's Champion.* Paducah, KY: Turner Publishing, 2001.

Montell, William. *Haunted Houses and Family Ghosts of Kentucky.* Lexington: University Press of Kentucky, 2001.

Mullins, Lashé D. and Charles K. *A History of White Hall: House of Clay.* Charleston, SC: The History Press, 2012.

CHAPTER 9: WHERE IS DANIEL BOONE BURIED?

Associated Press. "The Body in Daniel Boone's Grave May Not Be His." *New York Times,* July 21, 1983, pp. C13.

Benoit, Tod. *Where Are They Buried? How Did They Die?* New York: Black Dog & Leventhal Publishers, Inc., 2003.

Faragher, John Mack. *Daniel Boone: The Life and Legend of an American Pioneer.* New York: Henry Holt and Company, LLC, 1992.

Herman, Daniel J. "The Other Daniel Boone: The Nascence of a Middle-Class Hunter Hero, 1784–1860." *Journal of the Early Republic.* Autumn 1998, 18(3): pp. 429–457.

Lipton, Leah. "Chester Harding and the Life Portrait of Daniel Boone." *The American Art Journal.* Summer 1984, 16(3): pp. 4–19.

Lofaro, Michael. *Daniel Boone: An American Life.* Lexington: The University Press of Kentucky, 2003.

Spraker, Hazel Atterbury. *The Boone Family: A Genealogical History of the Descendants of George and Mary Boone.* Rutland, VT: The Tuttle Company Publishers, 1922.

Staten, Vince and Liz Baldi. *Kentucky Curiosities: Quirky Characters, Roadside Oddities & Other Offbeat Stuff.* Guilford, CT: Globe Pequot Press, 2003.

CHAPTER 10: THE CURSE OF ANNE MITCHELL

"General John Bell Hood: Myths and Realities." johnbellhood. org/myths.htm. Accessed December 24, 2012.

Gonsalves, Chris. *Haunted Love: Tales of Ghostly Soulmates, Spooky Suitors, and Eternal Love.* Guilford, CT: Globe Pequot Press, 2010.

O'Connor, Richard. "Anne's Curse," *LIFE* Magazine. October 25, 1948, p. 25.

Taylor, Troy. "John Bell Hood & the Curse of Anne Mitchell." militaryghosts.com/hood.html. Accessed December 23, 2012.

CHAPTER 11: EDGAR CAYCE: THE SLEEPING PROPHET

Breyerstein, Dale. "Edgar Cayce: The 'Prophet' Who 'Slept' His Way to the Top." *Skeptical Inquirer,* 1996, p. 32. www. gale.cengage.com. Accessed April 2, 2012.

Johnson, S. Laurence. "Edgar Cayce's Vision: The Golden Touch Part One." *Paraplegia News*, November 2000, 54(12): p. 16.

Johnson, S. Laurence. "Edgar Cayce's Vision: The Golden Touch Part Two." *Paraplegia News*, December 2000, 54(12): p. 28.

Kirkpatrick, Sidney. *Edgar Cayce: An American Prophet*. New York: Penguin Putnam, Inc., 2000.

Todeschi, Kevin. *Edgar Cayce on Vibrations: Spirit in Motion*. Virginia Beach, VA: A.R.E. Press, 2007.

CHAPTER 12: THE HAUNTING DEATH OF OCTAVIA HATCHER

"Battling the deadly bite of the tsetse fly," CNN.com. cnn.com/ HEALTH/9802/28/sudan.sleeping.sickness/. February 28, 1998. Accessed March 16, 2013.

Brown, Alan. *Haunted Kentucky: Ghosts and Strange Phenomena of the Bluegrass State*. Mechanicsburg, PA: Stackpole Books, 2009.

Connelley, William Elsey and E. M. Coulter, Ph.D. *History of Kentucky, Volume IV*. Chicago and New York: The American Historical Society, 1922.

Forsyth, Jessica. "The Story of Octavia Hatcher." appalachian history.net/2012/04/the-story-of-octavia-hatcher.html. April 3, 2012. Accessed March 16, 2013.

"Mystery Monday: Buried Alive." nikkibontv.com/tag/mystery-monday/. Video accessed March 16, 2013.

CHAPTER 13: THE SPIRITS OF WAVERLY HILLS SANATORIUM

Brown, Alan. *Ghost Hunters of the South*. Jackson: University Press of Mississippi, 2006.

Holland, Jeffrey Scott. *Weird Kentucky*. New York: Sterling Publishing Co., Inc., 2008.

Starr, Patti Accord. *Ghosthunting Kentucky*. Cincinnati, OH: Clerisy Press, 2010.

CHAPTER 14: THE MYSTERIES OF MAMMOTH CAVE

"A brief history of Mammoth Cave," National Park Service. nps. gov/maca/historyculture/abriefhistoryofmammothcave. htm. Accessed May 5, 2013.

"Mammoth Cave National Park Harbors More than a Few Ghost Stories." National Parks Traveler. October 30, 2009. nationalparkstraveler.com/2009/10/mammoth-cave-national-park-harbors-more-few-ghost-stories4820. Accessed May 5, 2013.

Sceurman, Mark and Mark Moran. *Weird Hauntings: True Tales of Ghostly Places*. New York: Sterling Publishing, 2006.

Taylor, Troy. "Mammoth Cave: The World's Largest Haunted Place." prairieghosts.com/mammoth.html. Accessed May 5, 2013.

GENERAL SOURCES

Harrison, Lowell and Klotter, James. *A New History of Kentucky*. Lexington: The University Press of Kentucky, 1997.

Kleber, John E. *The Kentucky Encyclopedia*. Lexington: The University Press of Kentucky, 1992.

INDEX